Comedy Writing Workbook

GENE PERRET

Sterling Publishing Co., Inc.   New York

To
Ed Hercer
who wouldn't let me stop
working out
even when things didn't seem to be
working out

Library of Congress Cataloging-in-Publication Data

Perret, Gene.
    Comedy writing workbook / by Gene Perret.
        p.   cm.
    ISBN 0-8069-6554-1
    1. Comedy—Authorship.   2. Wit and humor—Authorship.   I. Title.
PN6149.A88P46   1990   89-39963
808.7—dc20   CIP

Copyright © 1990 by Gene Perret
Published by Sterling Publishing Co., Inc.
387 Park Avenue South, New York, N.Y. 10016
Distributed in Canada by Sterling Publishing
% Canadian Manda Group, P.O. Box 920, Station U
Toronto, Ontario, Canada M8Z 5P9
Distributed in Great Britain and Europe by Cassell PLC
Artillery House, Artillery Row, London SW1P 1RT, England
Distributed in Australia by Capricorn Ltd.
P.O. Box 665, Lane Cove, NSW 2066
Manufactured in the United States of America

CONTENTS

BEFORE YOU BEGIN

This book is aptly titled. It is about writing comedy, and it will be work. That's why the projects in the book are called "workouts." They're meant to be challenging, to be exhausting, to exercise and develop your creative muscles.

The workouts aren't easy, but they're beneficial.

Comedy is deceptive. Done well, it appears almost effortless. But it's the effort that goes into it that produces the illusion. I'm a weekend tennis player and I often use sports—especially tennis—to illustrate what I mean. It's interesting that when I see still photos of the great tennis players, they always seem to be doing the proper thing. When I see still photos of me playing tennis, I look awkward. My racket is in the wrong position. My foot is where my hand should be. The ball is going in one direction, while I'm looking in the other.

That's because I'm usually off balance, but the pros play in perfect balance. They work out and practise so much that they've learned to outsmart the ball. They know where it's going, and their bodies are trained to get where they have to be. They swing with control and strike the ball properly.

Their hours of intensive training produce a swing that is smooth, fluid, effortless, and consequently more powerful and accurate.

Workouts such as those in this book are not reserved for the novice. When I worked on *The Carol Burnett Show*, I had lunch with one of the musicians in our orchestra. He told me he had to rush through lunch because he had to get to his lesson. I was intrigued because I assumed anyone who had reached his level would be giving lessons; not taking them.

I said. "You still take lessons?"

He said, "Of course."

I said, "Do you practise regularly?"

He said he did.

I asked, "How much?"

He said, "Oh, not too much anymore. Maybe four to six hours a day."

Four to six hours a day! That's an accomplished, top-level musician who was good enough to be in a studio orchestra. He still studied and practised regularly—up to six hours a day.

People who are good at what they do, practise. A baseball player may have his greatest year ever, but he still shows up for spring training the following season. The world champion in boxing still allows plenty of time for workouts in the gym before his next fight. Renowned ballerinas spend much more time in the practise studio than they do on the stage.

What do they practise? Basics. I saw David Robinson, the All-American from Navy, giving a basketball lesson once to some youngsters. He was teaching them to catch the ball. He suggested that they practise just throwing the ball back and forth to one another. "If you don't have anyone to catch with," he said, "throw the ball up against a wall just for the practise of catching it." What could be more basic than that? But that's why he recommended practising it. Robinson pointed out, "You can't go up for a slam dunk until you've caught the ball."

Almost all great accomplishments are born out of well-drilled fundamentals. Houses have to be built on firm foundations; skills have to be developed from basics.

There are two reasons for practice. One is to learn a new skill. We all experience that.

When we first learn to drive a car we don't know what to do or how to do it. We aren't sure we can steer or work the pedals. We practise and we learn.

Anyone who plays a musical instrument remembers struggling to get everything to work together—reading the notes, moving your fingers to the right place, getting your hands to do what your mind was telling them to do. It wasn't easy. Now you do all that with ease, probably not even thinking about what you're doing.

There are countless other examples—typing, knitting, mathematics. You know from experience that the more you do something, the better you get at it.

Another reason for practice, though, is to fine tune skills you already have—to go back and review basics.

I've always been a hacker on the golf course. If I break a hundred it's champagne for everybody. Most of the folks I play with are in the same class. It would always amuse me to see how our games could fluctuate. One playing partner would come out to the tee having just taken a lesson or read a new tip in the golf magazine. He'd concentrate so much on that pointer that he'd hit the ball magnificently—for about three holes.

Then he'd get cocky. He'd feel he knew all there was to know about golf. He'd start adding a little flourish to his follow-through. Then he'd being playing worse than he did before the lesson.

A good solid performance in any endeavor depends on all elements working together. If you allow any part of your performance to deteriorate, it can cause everything to collapse.

That's why you want to review your techniques periodically, and brush up on those that are lacking.

I once asked a tennis player while we were warming up before a match if he wanted me to hit him some lobs so he could practise his overhead smash. He said, "No, I never practise overheads because I'm lousy at them." Maybe he was "lousy" at them *because* he never practised them. If you spot a weakness in your skills, that's what you should attack with heavy-duty effort.

In my own writing work I sometimes notice that my jokes are getting too literal. I haven't been letting them blossom out into fanciful or wacky references. They're not zany enough. So I force myself to write some "crazy" gags.

Sometimes I get lazy and do the majority of my gags on the same subjects. That means I need to go back to basics and begin listing more references before I start the actual comedy writing.

You hear the same things from people in every profession. Chris Evert wins a tennis tournament but says she wants to work on improving her serve to get ready for Wimbledon. Jack Nicklaus wants to add some distance to his drives. A college team is ranked number one in the nation and the coach says he isn't happy with the team's defensive work.

Perfecting your craft is a never-ending duty. It's like properly maintaining a house. By the time you paint the outside, the inside needs wallpapering. After you clean up the backyard, the front lawn needs mowing. Keeping your skills in order is the same. It's a matter of constant checking and practising with workouts such as these.

Consistent practice, too, keeps your skills sharp. Once, when I was producing *Welcome Back, Kotter*, we had a scene that involved a school yard basketball game. I visited the set, and the performers on the show were shooting the basketball at the hoop we had set up on the stage. I used to be a fair basketball player when I was a kid—a good shooter. So I called for the ball. They couldn't refuse since I was the producer. I dribbled twice, threw the ball toward the basket, and missed by about five feet. The ball sailed over the backboard and knocked over some scenery on the next set.

Everyone laughed but me. I hadn't played basketball in 20 years, but I thought the eye and the coordination would be the same as it was when I was a kid. It wasn't. If skills aren't used, they disappear—to "skill heaven" or somewhere. Working out regularly is one way to keep them.

There's a fringe benefit to constant practice, too. It happens automatically. That bonus is experience.

There's no substitute for experience; there's no shortcut. You can't get it from reading or watching; you only get it from doing.

These workouts, though, are doing. Practice is doing. Therefore, the more time you spend practising, the more experience you have.

In your effort to succeed, your first duty is to be good, to learn your craft well. If your desire were to be a concert pianist, wouldn't it be wise for you to learn to play the piano?

Many variables affect your success, but perfecting your skills is one that you can control. You can study and practise whether you have connections in the business or not. Even if you can't get an audition or a tryout, you can still get better and better.

And if you get good enough—which is usually up to you—success can't hide from you. You have to make it.

Excellence is usually in short supply, but there is a high demand for it. If you have it, someone will find you.

How you use this book is completely up to you. The suggestions are on these pages, but the effort is your decision. You're the one who will decide how much effort to give to each workout. Of course, you're the one who will reap the benefits, too.

The workouts will certainly make demands on your time. This is not the kind of book that you read through and set aside. It may take many months to complete the exercises. Don't rush through. The benefit, remember, is not in completing them; it's in doing them.

Of course, you don't want to work through them too sluggishly, either. Sometimes postponing the work allows you to forget about it all together. These workouts serve no purpose unless you do them.

So set your own pace. Be demanding but not ridiculous with your scheduling. Take as much time as you need, but keep working. A consistent, steady work pace is more beneficial than a quick, "Get it out of the way and move on to the next one" routine.

I strongly recommend that the first time through this book, you do the workouts in order. Complete all the exercises in Chapter One before moving on to Chapter Two, Chapter Three, and so on. Don't skip any of them. Later, you can return to this book and redo the workouts in any order you like, but the first time through, do them all—in order.

I urge this for several reasons:

First, it's good discipline. If there's any trait that is an absolute requirement for a writer it's discipline—both in work habits and technique.

Second, doing all of the exercises in proper sequence eliminates the temptation to skip over those that are difficult or tedious. You might become like the tennis player who didn't want to practise overheads because he was lousy at them. You might say, "I don't want to work with words because I have a horrible vocabulary." That's exactly why you should do the workout on words.

Third, many of the workouts in the book depend upon both knowledge and material that you gathered from previous workouts. Attacking them out of sequence or skipping selected workouts would weaken the overall benefit of the book.

It is a workbook, so it will be work. Not much is ever accomplished without some effort. Sean O'Casey said, "When I stepped from hard manual work to writing, I just stepped from one kind of hard work to another." Toil, however, can seem less tedious when you're having fun.

Have fun with all the workouts.

Chapter One

WORKING WITH JOKES

I belong to a local tennis club. Most of the members compete at about the same relative level of mediocrity. Only once or twice a year do we all rise above our run-of-the-mill skill level. That's when the Wimbledon or U.S. Open matches are being shown on television.

After watching a few of those superb matches, we play above our heads. We sit home and view the powerful serve of Boris Becker, the finesse shots of John McEnroe, the explosive ground strokes of Ivan Lendl, the consistent passing shots of Chris Evert, and the athletic grace of Martina Navratilova; then we grab our rackets and a can of balls and come out and play a little bit more like those champions than we did last week.

Why? We play better for one of several reasons or a combination of all of them:

1. We learn technique. We see what the correct swing looks like. We observe the footwork, preparation, balance, and smooth effort that goes into a polished tennis stroke. Our mind remembers that and translates it into muscle memory. Rather than continue to make the rushed, awkward, flailing strokes that we made last week, we emulate the pros. Mechanically, we improve.

2. We absorb strategy. We normally play dumb; the professionals don't. They play the percentages. They play the shot that's going to make their next shot a winner. We amateurs go for a winner whether we have the opening or not. We blow a lot of easy shots by going for the unnecessary, more difficult shot. Watching the pros play smart eliminates many of our unintelligent shots.

3. These athletes play so darn well, that it's inspiring. It renews our enthusiasm for the game. We race out onto the court, eager for the competition. We're excited about playing the game; consequently, we play better.

4. We see the possibilities. We see the way the game should be played and realize that we, too, might be able to rip a passing shot down the line, or smash an overhead into the open court. We realize that we might be able to follow our serve into the net and put away a well-placed volley for a winning point. The despair of our mediocrity is replaced by the hope of improvement.

I've used tennis as an illustration, but the same phenomenon happens in all endeavors. Excellence is inspiring. It not only makes us want to emulate the masters, but it brings about improvement.

Understand—my neighbors and I don't rush onto the court and play like Jimmy Connors. Not at all. Being inspired doesn't automatically produce professional results. It does, though, bring about a certain level of improvement, a minimal improvement. Only practice, study, and dedicated effort can produce longer-lasting results— the kind that make champions.

However, that's another fringe benefit of watching the best: it can generate the passion we need to work hard at our craft. It can make us zealous enough to practise and perfect our technique, and perhaps eventually become as skillful as the masters we watch.

Even the professionals watch other professionals. Why? Because they learn from them, too. They keep current. They discover innovations.

To stay with our tennis example a little longer: years ago most top-level players hit all their shots one-handed. When young Chris Evert began learning the sport, she was so small that she couldn't handle the racket that well. So she swung at her backhand shots with two hands. It became a habit for her and she stayed with it. She ruled women's tennis for many years with that unorthodox swing. Others watched and decided to try it. Today, in the pro ranks there are just about as many top professionals using a two-handed backhand as there are using the more traditional one-handed swing.

These first few workouts are designed to get you to watch the masters of comedy. They're supposed to force you to notice the techniques, and the strategies that the best use.

By practising these workouts you'll see how they do what they do and why they do what they do. You'll be inspired, excited, and enthused by them.

You won't be doing much actual writing in these first few workouts. However, don't mistakenly conclude that because you're not putting pen to paper, these workouts are less important than the writing assignments that will come later in the book.

Of all the writing workouts, these first few are probably the most universally practised by professionals. I have asked many comedy writers what they do when they're not in the mood to write or when the assignment is not one that they want to attack. I wanted to know how they forced themselves to get to the word processor to complete their chores.

Most of them said they watched, listened to, or read the masters. One gentleman said, "I play just a few minutes of tape. I listen to the comedian I'm writing for. It only takes a few jokes of his to get me into his comedy timing and to inspire me. After that the jokes start flowing." Another watched videotapes for the same reason. A third writer said, "I go back and read some of the jokes I wrote for that same person a few months ago. It not only reminds me of that comedy rhythm, but it also convinces me that I wrote pretty good jokes then, and I can do it again."

The professionals in almost every field use this tactic.

So attack this first chapter of workouts with vigor. They'll improve your comedy writing immediately, and in the long run, they'll help you steadily improve your writing until it's of professional quality.

So let's get to it. Let's go to Wimbledon.

= WORKOUT 1A =
"My Collection of Favorite Jokes"

This is primarily a research workout. You'll get to read, look, and listen, to discover some of the good comedy that's being done by others.

HERE'S WHAT YOU DO FOR THIS WORKOUT

1. Gather a collection of 25 jokes that you think are top drawer. You want to find good, solid jokes that you would have been proud to have written; jokes that you would like in your own comedy act; jokes that you would show to others and say, "This is the kind of humor I aspire to."

You can listen to young comics on TV and jot down the lines that strike you. You can listen to the established legends of comedy—people like Bob Hope, Milton Berle, Johnny Carson—and note some of their outstanding gags. You can research lines in magazines or books. You can pull them from your own memory—lines you've heard and remembered over the years. You can even jot down lines that you hear second-hand. Someone says, "Did you hear what Carson said last night?" When they tell you the joke (and they will), if it's one that you consider worthy of your list, write it down.

2. Get your 25 exemplary jokes on paper. If you clip them, you can staple them to a file card or a sheet of paper. You can type them or scribble them out by hand. It is important, though, that you get them on paper and save them because you may want to use a few of these examples in later workouts. Also jot down the name of the comedian. You'll see later that it might be beneficial to your own comedy.

3. After each gag you collect, write a brief reason why it made your "personal favorite" list. You needn't be too clinical—just a top-of-the-head evaluation. Why did *you* like *this* joke?

HERE'S WHAT THIS WORKOUT WILL DO FOR YOU

This workout will open your eyes, ears, all of your senses and all your sensibilities to the world of humor. You'll be more attuned to the comedic. You'll hear more funny lines, remember more, and file more ideas into your memory for later use.

I've always been fascinated in watching sports on television at how sharp-eyed some of the commentators are. When I watch bowling, I just see the pins "explode." The commentator, though, tells you exactly where each pin went. When I watch diving, I don't know how many turns and spins that diver took. My eye can't follow it. But the commentators know.

It's not that their eyes are sharper or quicker; it's just that they know what to look for, how to look for it, and where to look. They're tuned in to that sport. You can acquire a similar awareness with humor.

Also, you'll be more aware of what other writers are doing—not only the lines and types of jokes they're doing, but what they're talking about. You'll notice what they're observing in the world around them, and you may begin noticing similar topics that are ripe for humor.

You'll uncover interesting things about your own tastes and sense of humor. You may discover you like comics that you dismissed earlier. You may be surprised to learn that the type of jokes you prefer are not the ones you thought you would.

With 25 jokes to study and analyze, you'll begin to uncover patterns. Those trends will indicate the direction in which your own comedy style should move.

You'll recognize how good the best humorists can be (They're not always great, but when they are, they're magnificent). It will give you a goal to shoot for in your own work. You won't be as ready to settle for mediocre after seeing how good it can get.

HERE ARE SOME EXAMPLES

These are ten of my favorite jokes, with a short explanation and analysis of each one. This should give you an idea of how the workout works and what this list shows about my comedy style.

★   ★   ★   ★   ★

1. Bob Hope did this line when America was having trouble with its space program. Each rocket we fired failed and fell into the ocean. The Russians had already successfully launched Sputnik, but we hadn't yet sent a rocket into space. On the day of the Bob Hope telecast, another launch had just aborted into the Atlantic Ocean. He said:

"Well, I guess you heard the good news from Cape Canaveral. The United States just launched another submarine."

I like this for several reasons. First it was topical. The event just happened that day and everyone was talking about it. Second, it was great audience misdirection. We all thought the news from Cape Canaveral was *bad* news; he said it was good. Our ears perked up to find out what was good about it. Third, the punchline was kept hidden until the very last word—submarine. That one word changed the meaning of the entire statement.

★   ★   ★   ★   ★

2. Johnny Carson did this line on the night of the giant earthquake that hit the Los Angeles area in 1971. He opened his show that night by saying:

"The 'God is Dead' meeting that was scheduled for tonight, has been cancelled."

Again, it was topical, just a few hours old. And it was being talked about. It said by implication that all those folks who experienced the quake said a little prayer, whether they ever prayed before or not.

★   ★   ★   ★   ★

3. Will Rogers was asked about his political affiliation. He said:

"I belong to no organized political party. I'm a Democrat."

I love the way this line leads the audience in one direction and then tricks them. The first sentence is a standard cop-out from someone who doesn't want to reveal his politics. Then he changes it with the second sentence. He is saying in effect, "I'm a Democrat, but they're not organized."

★   ★   ★   ★   ★

4. Jay Leno said:

"Did you read where this is National Condom Week? Hey now, there's a parade you won't want to miss."

I love this line because it creates such a bizarre image. It's topical, but that's not the important part of this joke. It's also a little naughty, but not offensive. I think it's a bright comment that paints a funny picture.

★　　★　　★　　★　　★

5. Phyllis Diller said:

"My husband, Fang, drinks too much. He cut himself shaving this morning, and he bled so bad his eyes cleared up."

This joke paints a delightful graphic image. It says that his eyes were bloodshot without really saying it. It implies it.

★　　★　　★　　★　　★

6. Here's a Rodney Dangerfield classic:

"My father gave me a bat for Christmas. First time I tried to play with it, it flew away."

I like this one because of the silly picture it paints, too. But this one also tricks the audience. Practically everyone thinks of a baseball bat, then the last few words tell us that it was a bat that lives in a cave. It's a goofy gift for a father to give a son. Funny joke.

★　　★　　★　　★　　★

7. Jackie Mason had a line that went something like the following. I'm paraphrasing:

"My grandfather always told me, "Don't look after your money; look after your health." One day I was looking after my health, I found out my money was gone. My grandfather took it."

It's a longer style of joke, but it misdirects the audience. All of us believe in the grandfatherly advice that we get from the older generation. They seem so wise, and that's the way Jackie Mason paints his grandpa. It's not until the last four words that we realize the old geezer was a crook. We've been fooled and we laugh.

★　　★　　★　　★　　★

8. I loved this Henny Youngman joke. Again I'm reconstructing it from memory:

"My son kept coming to me every day complaining about headaches. Every day—headaches, headaches, headaches. I said to him, 'How many times do I have to tell you? When you get out of the bed in the morning, feet first.' "

I like it because it's a funny picture and because you never see the punchline coming. None of us would guess that the kid dives out of bed each morning and lands on the floor on his head. But it's logical. If he did that, he'd have a headache.

★　　★　　★　　★　　★

9. Phyllis Diller has a line about her mother-in-law, a large lady she calls "Moby Dick."

"Moby Dick gave me one of her old dresses the other day. I plan to have it starched and made into a summer home."

I love the image this joke creates, and the fact that you can't see the punchline coming. You wonder what good one of those old dresses would be, then the comic gives you a zany, but logical use for it.

★   ★   ★   ★   ★

10. This last is a Phyllis Diller line, too. It kids her bad cooking. She tells about the time a "grease fire broke out in my sink":

"The firemen put it out quickly, but three of them had to be treated for food inhalation."

I like this one because the punchline is perfectly disguised. Up until the last two words, it's a normal statement. Substituting "food inhalation" for "smoke inhalation" turns the sentence completely around. It surprises the listeners; it makes it funny.

A WORD BEFORE YOU START

You can readily see from my list that I like the short, meaningful one-liners. I tend more to the Bob Hope, Jay Leno, Phyllis Diller, Joan Rivers style than to someone like Robin Williams.

I like gags that set the audience up for one thing and then turn the tables on them, misdirect them.

I also like gags that create outlandish images in the minds of the listeners.

You'll be able to see patterns in your own comedy preferences as you do your own organized analysis of your selection. For example, you may find yourself drawn to the bizarre, way-out style of a Stephen Wright, or maybe the flakiness of a Gracie Allen or Tom Smothers. You might prefer the colorful story style of Bill Cosby or the frenetic, frantic pace of Robin Williams.

There are many styles of comedy to select from. This workout will help you zero in on your favorite.

So begin your search, and have fun with it.

= WORKOUT 1B =
"My Collection of Favorite Quotes"

This workout is largely research, too. It might involve even more extensive research than Workout 1A. You're going to be looking for one-liners that have withstood the test of time. You want to find some classic, but funny, quotes.

HERE'S WHAT YOU DO FOR THIS WORKOUT

1. Assemble a collection of 25 attributable quotes on the following subjects:

Sex	Friends
Death	Virtue
Laughter	Acting
Cynicism	Writing
Gossip	Health
Marriage	Wealth
Courtship	Intellectuals
War	(real or supposed)

There are 15 different topics. Find at least one quote on each topic; the remaining 10 you can distribute in any fashion you like.

Use a reference book for your research. Don't rely on your memory. First, memory can be inaccurate. You may remember the wording differently from the original, and it's the original that holds the lesson.

Second, in looking up the quote, you will read and consider many other quotes. The ones you don't choose can be as helpful in the learning process as those you do.

2. Assemble your collection of quotes, along with the authors' names, on paper. Save them. You may want to use them in later workouts.

HERE'S WHAT THIS WORKOUT WILL DO FOR YOU

These epigrams, aphorisms, quotes, sayings, and other one-liners, have been preserved for posterity. Some of them may be hundreds of years old. They've survived because they're worthwhile.

As you read through them for your research and select your favorites, you'll be learning something about those quotes. What made them noteworthy in the first place? What made them so remarkable that they have lasted this long?

Most of these sayings are more than funny. They say something. In reading through them, analyzing them, selecting several, and studying your selections, you'll begin to see how to combine wit with wisdom.

In researching specific topics you'll see how others have dissected that topic. As you first read through the 15 topics mentioned earlier, you may think there is nothing witty or worthwhile to say about some of them. When you see how other minds have commented on that topic, you'll learn that there are many approaches to each subject, and many facets to each topic.

HERE ARE SOME EXAMPLES

In the workout I didn't ask you to comment on why you chose certain quotes, so I won't comment either. Most of these lines are so strong that they don't need any elaboration.

Sex:

"Familiarity breeds contempt . . . and children."

—*Mark Twain*

★　★　★　★　★

Death:

"It's not that I'm afraid to die, I just don't want to be there when it happens."

—*Woody Allen*

★　★　★　★　★

Laughter:

"He who laughs has not yet heard the bad news."

—*Bertolt Brecht*

★　★　★　★　★

Cynicism:

"A cynic is a man who when he smells flowers, looks around for a coffin."

—*H. L. Mencken*

★　★　★　★　★

Gossip:

"If you can't say something good about someone, sit right here by me."

—*Alice Roosevelt Longworth*

★　★　★　★　★

Marriage:

"Marriage is a great institution; but I'm not ready for an institution."

—*Mae West*

★　★　★　★　★

Courtship:

"She was a lovely girl. Our courtship was fast and furious—I was fast and she was furious."

—*Max Kauffmann*

★　★　★　★　★

War:

"War is only a cowardly escape from the problems of peace."

—*Thomas Mann*

★　★　★　★　★

Friends:

"Your friend is the man who knows all about you, and still likes you."

—*Elbert Hubbard*

★　★　★　★　★

Virtue:

"What, after all, is a halo? It's only one more thing to keep clean."

—*Christopher Fry*

★　★　★　★　★

Acting:
  "The important thing in acting is to be able to laugh and cry. If I have to cry, I think of my sex life. If I have to laugh, I think of my sex life."
  —*Glenda Jackson*

★　　★　　★　　★　　★

Writing:
  "What is a writer but a schmuck with an Underwood."
  —*Jack Warner*

★　　★　　★　　★　　★

Health:
  "Be careful about reading health books. You may die of a misprint."
  —*Mark Twain*

★　　★　　★　　★　　★

Wealth:
  "Nouveau is better than no riche at all."

  —*Monsieur Marc*

★　　★　　★　　★　　★

Intellectuals (real or supposed):
  "People who refer to themselves as intellectuals are automatically committing a social crime and, also, usually an error."
  —*Tracy Young*

★　　★　　★　　★　　★

Start your research and have fun looking.

= WORKOUT 1C =
"My Collection of My Favorite's Favorites"

This research workout will be more fun because it's custom designed to your taste in comedy. Workouts 1A and 1B extended your comedy awareness. They forced you to read and listen to other humorists to get you out of your comfortable comedy rut. Now Workout 1C lets you back into that "comfort zone."

HERE'S WHAT YOU DO FOR THIS WORKOUT

1. Select one comedian or humorist that you especially like. You may have many favorites. If so, you can do this workout several times. However, each time you do it, limit yourself to one specific mentor.

2. Collect 25 of your comic's (or humorist's) outstanding lines—those lines you consider best. Do this by reading books or magazine articles about your mentor, by listening to tapes of TV appearances, or by jotting down lines that you recall.

3. Get those lines on paper and save them. We will use them in future workouts.

HERE'S WHAT THIS WORKOUT WILL DO FOR YOU

Comedy is subjective. You may like Comic A while someone else doesn't see anything funny in him. Someone else may like Comic B, who doesn't make you laugh. There are reasons why you like certain comics, but you may not even know what those reasons are.

This workout will filter out the best lines from your favorite performers or writers. Listing them, studying them, and analyzing them will teach you quite a bit about their comedy styles. It will also reveal considerable information about your own comedy tastes and preferences.

As much as you like some particular performers and would like to emulate their work, your style will remain different from theirs. This workout will teach you even more about yourself than it does about your favorite performers.

Also, it often makes sense in the beginning of your writing to emulate a favorite. Bob Hope admits that he began by imitating vaudevillian Frank Fay. There is a lot of Jack Benny in Johnny Carson's work. When Richard Pryor was a young comedian, he looked like a clone of Bill Cosby. Yet all of these performers went on to develop their own individual comedy characterizations.

Studying and copying another's style doesn't inhibit your individuality; it enhances it. It lets you know that you're headed in the right direction. It develops good writing techniques. Eventually, you add your own flair to those techniques. That develops a new style—your style.

Studying someone you admire helps you develop it more quickly.

HERE ARE SOME EXAMPLES

I've selected Bob Hope as my mentor. I chose him not only for the purposes of this short example in Workout 1C, but because I chose him as my mentor when I was a beginning writer.

I would tape Bob Hope's television monologues, type them out and study them.

Then a week or so later, I chose different topics from the daily papers and tried to duplicate the form of Hope's monologue with the different subjects. It was great practice and I recommend it.

Here are a few of his lines that I especially like:

"You're only as young as you feel. When I get up in the morning, I don't feel anything until noon. By then it's time for my nap."

* * * * *

"I go for a swim every single day. It's either that or buy a new golf ball."

* * * * *

"I think travel is very educational. I can now say 'Kaopectate' in seven different languages."

* * * * *

"When I was a kid I slept in one bed with six brothers. We had one bed-wetter. It took us two years to find out who it was."

* * * * *

"I like politicians who pray a lot. It keeps their hands up where we can see them."

* * * * *

"I always carry tranquilizers with me when I fly. The hard part is getting the stewardesses to take them."

* * * * *

"I have the perfect simplified tax form for our government. Why don't they just print our money with a return address on it?"

* * * * *

"I had a flight attendant on the last flight who was so old, after she demonstrated the oxygen mask she left it on."

* * * * *

"We've had a lot of mudslides in California lately. I was driving to work the other day, glanced out the window, and my house was making better time than I was."

* * * * *

"I like to play golf with Jerry Ford. You don't have to keep score; you just look back along the fairway and count the wounded."

* * * * *

(When he spoke about the fire at his house in Palm Springs):
"It's a terrible feeling to wake up one morning and find out that the black cloud hanging over Los Angeles used to be your home in Palm Springs."

* * * * *

(In reply to the question: "How's your golf game?")
"If it was a boxing match, they'd stop it."

There's a fantastic dozen that should tell much about my comedy preferences. Your selection will educate you about your style, too. Dig those lines out and have fun doing it.

= WORKOUT 1D =
"My Collection of Favorite Cartoons"

This workout is largely research, too. It's similar to the other workouts in Chapter One except that it adds another element—the visual.

HERE'S WHAT YOU DO FOR THIS WORKOUT

1. Assemble a collection of 25 cartoons that you consider first-rate. You can get them from magazines, newspapers, or cartoon collections. It will be hard to gather these from your memory because you should have the drawing, too. For our purposes here, the graphic image is as important as the caption.

2. Get your outstanding cartoons on paper just as you did in Workout 1A. Save these, too, because you may use them in later workouts.

3. After each cartoon, write a brief reason for selecting it. What made this joke funny, or meaningful for you?

HERE'S WHAT THIS WORKOUT WILL DO FOR YOU

Comedy rarely works in a vacuum. In today's visual age, with television, films, video-cassettes, and even live performances, an audience doesn't just "hear" comedy; they "see" it. The lines are important, but so is the scenery, the action, the mannerisms of the performers, the "takes." Jack Benny often got his biggest laughs from his reaction to the comedy lines rather than from the lines themselves.

Workout 1A uncovered some classic comedy lines. They were lines that were quotable, lines that could stand alone and be funny. This workout shows us that humor can tie into actions or settings. It shows us that a line doesn't always have to be funny on its own; it can be funny in relation to its surroundings.

This workout will show you how the words must complement the action to produce the humor. It will demonstrate how the action can sometimes enhance the humor of the words, and conversely, how the words sometimes influence the action.

It also points out the importance of "captioning." In this case, the captions are connected with a drawing, but in humor we can caption many things—a straight line, for instance. We can caption an incident, a headline, a person. It's an important technique in writing and performing comedy. This workout studies it in its basic form.

HERE ARE SOME EXAMPLES

Here are a few of my favorite cartoons. Ideally, the artwork should be included here, too, but these are cartoons that I saw years ago and preserved only in my memory. I don't think you'll have any trouble, though, *visualizing the drawings.*

1. Two men are chained to and suspended from a dreary prison wall. They have obviously been there for some time because they are scrawny and their clothes are tattered. They are chained hand and foot, completely immobilized, and totally help-less. One turns to the other and whispers:

"Here's my plan."

I like this because it reminds me of so many people like this—people who try the silliest things in the face of overwhelming odds. The caption carries this idea to the ultimate. The drawing clearly shows that no one could ever be more helpless than these two, yet the one guy still has an idea that he thinks might work.

★　　★　　★　　★　　★

2. A sleepy father in pajamas and slippers is passing the room where his two sons are sound asleep with two large dogs on the bed with them. The Dad has tossed a cat in, and the drawing catches the cat in mid-flight. There is terror in the cat's eyes, and his hair is standing on end. The dad simply says:

"Time to get up, boys."

I like this one because it begins a story that the reader must finish. Anyone looking at that cartoon knows that all hell is going to break loose when that cat lands in the vicinity of those dogs. The reader will write his own funny material in his own mind.

★　　★　　★　　★　　★

3. This drawing shows cattle as far as the eye can see. They are grazing peacefully on the hillside—except for two who are in the foreground. They look sneaky. Their heads are lowered and their eyes seem to be scanning the surrounding area. One whispers to the other:

"The stampede's at midnight. Pass it on."

I like this because it's so wacky, so zany. To me, it's a funny idea that cattle actually plan stampedes the way prisoners plan breaks. The devious look in the eyes of those steers made the cartoon a gem.

★　　★　　★　　★　　★

4. This cartoon shows two men suspended from a dungeon wall, chained there by the wrists. One of the men has been there quite some time. He has tattered clothing, long hair and a beard. The other gentleman looks rather sprightly. He is a well-dressed court jester. Obviously, he's just been chained in the cell. With obvious enthusiasm, he says to the veteran prisoner:

"I had 'em rolling in the aisles until I inadvertently mentioned the Queen's moustache."

Frankly, I like this one because it has to do with the comedy profession. However, I think it's a great joke even aside from that. I can almost see the backstory, the incidents that lead up to his being chained in a dungeon. He was going good. He had everyone laughing, then he got carried away. He said something he shouldn't have. The Queen stopped laughing. With just a few words and expressions on cartoon faces, an entire comic short story comes alive in my mind.

★　　★　　★　　★　　★

5. This one shows a knight sitting on a bench in battle mail. Beside him sits a court jester. The knight says:

"I don't see how you ever think 'em up."

As a joke writer, I hear that comment many times. Seeing it in a cartoon fractured me. It's not so funny aside from that. However, that's a valid lesson, too. Humor has added impact when it hits the audience squarely between the eyes.

A WORD BEFORE YOU START

Notice the punchlines in these cartoons that I selected. They are:

"Here's my plan."

"Time to get up, boys."

"The stampede's at midnight. Pass it on."

"I had 'em rolling in the aisles until I inadvertently mentioned the Queen's moustache."

"I don't see how you ever think 'em up."

Not one of them is funny on its own. Each of them works in partnership with a scene, a setting, an action. This is the same type of cooperation that we see in films, stage plays, and teleplays.

In Workout 1A, all the lines, except for some minimal background, stood alone. These lines don't. We've seen two different styles of humor in these two workouts.

As you complete this workout, analyze the results, and compare them to Workout 1A, you'll develop more of a feel for your style of comedy writing.

Begin your research and have fun.

Chapter Two

WORKING WITH WORDS

I once watched an interview with Andres Segovia, the great classical guitarist. The interviewer asked Segovia about his guitar, where it was made and by whom, what type of strings he preferred, how he cared for the instrument. The Maestro spoke so lovingly about his guitar that the listeners began to accept it as a person, a friend.

The interviewer must have felt that way, also, because he asked if he might pick it up, hold it, perhaps even strum it once or twice. Segovia said, "No." He offered no explanation, no clumsy rationalization; he simply said no.

It was a shocking moment at first because Segovia seemed almost rude. Then the logic of his reply sank in. This was Segovia's instrument. With it, he established his fame, he changed the world of guitar, he brought his music to his fans. Segovia cared for this guitar and only Segovia would play this guitar.

That was his instrument; words are our instruments. Writers have to embrace language with the same consideration that Segovia had for his guitar. We have to become as familiar with the shadings and nuances of words as the Maestro was with the frets on his fingerboard. We have to study vocabulary and even listen to dialects.

It's true that ideas are the heart of comedy, but words are the device we use to transmit our ideas. The better we use words, the more accurately and graphically we're able to convey our ideas, our humor.

To see how words can be used to express an idea concisely and powerfully, read almost any page of Shakespeare. To learn how effectively words can be used to express comedy, read almost any quote from Woody Allen. Allen's grammar and language are so precise that they're almost impossible to improve. The words he uses are not only the words that should be used, but they seem absolutely necessary for the humor. You feel that the joke might not work if different words were used.

Words are the humorist's connection with the audience. We try to take ideas from our minds and put them into their minds, but there is no interface for doing that directly. We do it mostly through dialogue. Therefore, knowing how to use language well serves us well.

Familiarity with the language gives us more comedic options. That's why writers use a thesaurus. They want to find the word that comes as close as possible to saying what they mean. The words listed in the thesaurus give them more options. So when you're looking for a clever phrase, the more you know about language, the more selections you have available.

Second, facility with words helps us to tell our humorous stories better. We can make our points more accurately and clearly; we can make them more visually interesting, and with more colorful imagery.

As we develop a good working knowledge of language, we can use the inherent nuances in words to enhance the subtlety of our comedy ideas.

The pen is mightier than the sword, but only if we work hard to keep it sharper.

The following workouts will give you an appreciation for the playfulness of the English language, and help you learn how to use it to complement your own sense of humor.

So let's get to them. Make way for the Segovias of comedy.

WORKING WITH WORDS 25

= WORKOUT 2A =
"A Rose by Any Other Name"

If a softball pitcher delivers an underhand pitch, it means that he or she is throwing the ball legally. That's the way the rules say you must pitch in softball. If a business person makes an underhand deal, it means he or she is doing something illegal or unethical. Same word, same spelling, totally different meaning.

This workout will reveal how deceptive the English language can be. Words that seem to mean one thing can mean something else. Words that appear to have an obvious definition, can have several hidden meanings, too.

It will also point out how flexible words can be. We can use different meanings at different times or different meanings at the same time.

HERE'S WHAT YOU DO FOR THIS WORKOUT

Find at least five different, yet legitimate definitions for the following 20 words.

bear	deck	hit	plot	show
carriage	delivery	horse	seat	track
cart	finger	house	shoe	well
cup	heart	place	shoot	window

Some of the definitions may indicate totally different meanings. For example, the word "play" can mean to engage in some exercise for amusement. It can also mean a theatrical presentation. Those are two valid yet totally different definitions of the word "play."

It can also mean a strategy as in a baseball game ("The team put on a play.") or it can mean an athletic feat ("What a great fielding play.") The last two definitions are similar but with a slight shade of difference. Both are acceptable.

Use some slang if it's readily recognized and in general use. However, compound forms of the word aren't allowed. For example, "play money" is the same as "play," meaning pretend or make-believe.

Try to find at least five acceptable definitions for each word. With a little more effort, you can probably uncover seven meanings. With some struggle and creativity, you may be able to come up with as many as ten or more.

HERE'S WHAT THIS WORKOUT WILL DO FOR YOU

This workout will show you some of the nuances of the English language, and how words can be tricky, playful, and useful in creating comedy.

It will also indicate the depth of meaning that exists in seemingly simple words, and will show you the power you have to explore those hidden meanings.

HERE ARE SOME EXAMPLES

I've chosen the word "fly." It's a simple word, and you may have come up with several definitions by simply reading the word.

   1. to soar through the air under control, as a bird does

2. to travel by airplane

3. to cause something to float on air currents, as in "fly a kite"

Note: Some may argue that these are all the same meaning, but they aren't when you're actually using them. A bird flying to Pittsburgh is much different than you flying to Pittsburgh. In fact, there's an old joke, based on this difference, that night-club comics used to use:

"Ladies and gentlemen, I just flew in from Pittsburgh, and, boy, are my arms tired!"

And the verbs in definition 1 and definition 3 are different in that one is passive and one is active. The kite is flying, but you are flying the kite.

4. a winged insect

5. a ball hit into the air

6. the front opening in a pair of trousers

7. a type of fishing lure

8. the area above a stage or proscenium

9. to lift people or scenery in stage lingo. "To fly the scenery" is to lift it off the stage and hide it in the area out of view above the stage. "To fly performers" is to lift them into the air and suspend them above the stage.

10. to travel or run fast, as in "They were flying down the highway."

11. to gather momentum, as in "I started slow, but I'm really flying now."

12. to pass swiftly, as in "Time flies."

13. to avoid or shun, as in "to fly from trouble"

14. a disease in turnips

15. a hackney carriage

16. the outer canvas of a tent

17. the frame that takes the sheets from the cylinder of a printing press.

A WORD BEFORE YOU START

I wasn't sure that I could find even five definitions when I selected the word "fly." Yet, there are 17 legitimate, acceptable meanings for that three-letter word. Granted, a few of them are obscure and I did need a dictionary to uncover them, but most of them are familiar to all of us.

A comedian a few years ago gave a good example of how we can use these meanings to generate comedy. In his stage act, he sang a few lines from the song, "Volare," which was popular at the time. Then he said:

"Volare . . . that means 'fly' in Italian. It's very important that you know that, because some day you might be walking along the streets of Italy, and a stranger approaches you and says, 'Excuse me, sir, but your volare is open.' "

Approach this workout with enthusiasm, and don't surrender too easily. Investigate and find as many meanings for each word as you can.

Have fun with it.

= WORKOUT 2B =
"Mrs. Malaprop's Affliction"

In the previous workout we saw how one word can have different—sometimes contradictory—meanings. In this workout we'll see that one meaning can often have several words assigned to it. These are malapropisms.

A malapropism is a ridiculous misuse of words, usually through the confusion caused by a resemblance in sound. For instance, someone might say, "I was feeling peppy when I woke up this morning, but now I'm beginning to feel a little dyspeptic." "Dyspeptic" in this instance is being used to mean "not peppy." It may sound like that, but it doesn't mean that.

Of course, we all know the meaning of the words, "in alphabetical order," right? Wrong. Consider Casey Stengel's instructions to his players at spring training: "I want you all to line up in alphabetical order, according to your size."

Again, we see that words are tricky—they're playful. They can sound like they mean a certain thing when they really don't. In many cases, the "sound-alike" meaning can be more graphic than the real meaning. In writing comedy, we can take advantage of this phenomenon.

In this workout, you'll be creating humorous malapropisms of your own, beginning from scratch.

HERE'S WHAT YOU DO FOR THIS WORKOUT

Write 25 humorous sentences where the humor comes from the misinterpretation of a word. The comedy may come from simply inserting a similar-sounding word for the correct word. For instance, a boxer who says, "I want to be the champion. With me that's almost an abstention." A more advanced type of comedy may be generated when the wrong word not only sounds like the correct word it replaces, but also gives an ironic meaning to the sentence. For example, if the same fighter said "To be the heavyweight champion is a goal to which I perspire."

In another type of misinterpretation the explanation of the word doesn't correspond with the word. That's the "alphabetical order according to size" type.

You can attack this workout from any direction you like: Turn to the dictionary, or a rhyming dictionary, for sound-alike words. Or begin with the correct word and try to find another that sounds like it or seems to have a similar meaning, but doesn't.

Create examples of each type of humor: The pure misuse of sound-alike words; then the sound-alike word that generates a different meaning; and finally, the definition that contradicts the meaning.

The example section of this workout lists more illustrations of all three types.

HERE'S WHAT THIS WORKOUT WILL DO FOR YOU

This workout will force you to investigate the meanings of words and their nuances. You'll begin to look beyond the obvious meaning of a given word to find both hidden meanings and meanings that you might create—meanings that the word could have based on its spelling or sound.

Looking beyond the obvious is good training for a comedy writer—not only with words, but also with ideas.

This workout will teach you to associate one idea with another. When you find the given word, you are forced to search for sound-alikes. "Deter" could sound like "inter," "intern," "defer," "detour," "demure" and who-knows-how-many others.

Searching for related words and meanings is good practice for later workouts when you'll be searching for related ideas and concepts as the basis of your humor.

HERE ARE SOME EXAMPLES

The first examples are simply misused words. They sound like the right word, but they aren't. They're basically examples of "stupid" humor. That is, the person saying them doesn't know that they are wrong. They don't give any new meaning to the sentences.

1. "If I do you a favor I would expect that you precipitate."
The speaker here meant to say "reciprocate."

★   ★   ★   ★   ★

2. "The boss called me in and told me my services were being exterminated."
The speaker meant "terminated."

★   ★   ★   ★   ★

3. "I've loved writing comedy ever since I was in my infantry."

I think this person enjoyed writing since he was a small child; not since he served in the army. He meant to say "infancy."

★   ★   ★   ★   ★

The next examples show a word that sounds right but is wrong. However, that wrong word gives a different twist, a funny twist, to the original sentence.

4. "The parson gave such a great sermon that the congregation gave him a standing donation."

"Ovation" is the correct word here, but perhaps the parson would have preferred a "donation."

★   ★   ★   ★   ★

5. "I was such a great lover on my honeymoon that my wife gave me a standing ovulation."

"Ovation" again is the proper word, but the incorrect word definitely changes the meaning, and the humor content, of this sentence.

★   ★   ★   ★   ★

6. "I was on my best behavior with this blind date. I think I made a terrific first depression on the girl."

"Terrific first impression" connotes a positive reaction; "terrific first depression" is much different. This is funny because the man obviously thinks he did well, but what he is saying probably is closer to the truth.

The last examples are malapropisms in which the speaker seems completely oblivious to the meaning of the key words in the sentence—but each one makes its point!

★   ★   ★   ★   ★

7. Samuel Goldwyn is reported to have said this: "A verbal agreement isn't worth the paper it's written on."

It's hard to tell which Mr. Goldwyn was misusing, the phrase "verbal agreement," or the proverbial "paper it's written on."

★　　★　　★　　★　　★

8. The Commanding officer announced, "Dress uniforms this evening will be strictly optional, and that's an order."

I don't know precisely what he meant, but I'd wear my dress uniform just to be safe.

★　　★　　★　　★　　★

9. "Anyone who is absent from tonight's meeting will be sent home immediately."

Pretty severe punishment for someone who isn't even there. I wonder if they will be physically carried out by the Sergeant-at-Arms?

A WORD BEFORE YOU START

Well, you get the idea. Cram as much new meaning into your misinterpreted meanings as possible. This workout can lead to some bizarre statements!

Have fun with it.

= WORKOUT 2C =
"The Dictionary Must Be Wrong"

Words are mischievous, too, in that many times they're not the sum of their parts. For instance, "defile" means to insult, to soil, to tarnish; however, it sounds like the file drawer that you'd find between the C-file and the E-file.

Comedy writers can capitalize on this playfulness that's built into the language. We can use either the literal definition or the sound-alike meaning.

In this workout we'll explore this phenomenon.

HERE'S WHAT YOU DO FOR THIS WORKOUT

Create 20 meanings for readily-recognizable words that are incorrect, but logical. You may select any words you like; in fact, finding the right word is the major part of the workout. Naturally, you create the comedic definition, too. For example, "profile" is a filing cabinet that has lost its amateur standing; and "debate" is something you use to catch de fish with.

HERE'S WHAT THIS WORKOUT WILL DO FOR YOU

This workout forces you to explore new areas of vocabulary—to stretch, to expand, to think of words that you don't often use. Investigating new vocabulary frontiers is always beneficial to a writer.

Also, this workout helps you to look beyond the obvious. You'll be analyzing words that you're familiar with, but you'll be giving them unfamiliar definitions, new meanings. Looking beyond the obvious is always good practice for a comedy writer.

This is good practice, too, in searching out relationships. You'll be working from a "known" and searching out another "known" that relates to it. That's a great way to teach the mind to think funny, relating one idea with another.

HERE ARE SOME EXAMPLES

Here are several ordinary words to which I've assigned new and wacky definitions:

beleaguered: a baseball player who will never make it to the major leagues.

★ ★ ★ ★ ★

debase: what you slide into when you steal second

★ ★ ★ ★ ★

debunk: the technical term for pushing a sailor out of bed.

★ ★ ★ ★ ★

deduce: de card in de deck between de ace and de trey.

★ ★ ★ ★ ★

diatribe: what you do when you change the color of a whole group of Indians at the same time.

★ ★ ★ ★ ★

intense: where Lawrence of Arabia kept his soldiers.

★ ★ ★ ★ ★

pragmatic: an electronic machine that makes prags.

★ ★ ★ ★ ★

snapdragon: a mythical lizard-like animal whose religious beliefs forbid the use of either buttons or zippers.

★ ★ ★ ★ ★

squire: an equilateral rectangle with a decidedly Cockney accent.

A WORD BEFORE YOU START

Notice the variations in these examples. "Debase" and "debunk" are pretty much the same. "De" became a colloquial mispronunciation of the word "the." However, in "deduce," the mispronunciation was incorporated into the definition, too. "Diatribe" gives new meanings to a couple of the syllables in the word.

The definition of the word "pragmatic" created an entirely new word—"prag." I don't know what a prag is, but if there were a machine that electronically made them, it would probably be called a "pragmatic."

The "snapdragon" definition evoked a creature with religious convictions, and "squire" conjures up the bizarre image of the thing being defined pronouncing itself.

So you can see that even though this workout limits itself to working with words, it nevertheless stimulates inventiveness and comic creativity.

You'll have some fun with it.

= WORKOUT 2D =
"So You Wanna Be Noah Webster"

This workout is similar to Workout 2C, except that it approaches from a different direction. In this case, you'll have to manufacture a reasonably logical definition for a word that you don't know the meaning of. Therefore, your only frame of reference will be the sound of the syllables or your assumed meaning of them.

HERE'S WHAT YOU DO FOR THIS WORKOUT

1. Search through the dictionary for ten words that you don't know the definition of—and don't look at the definition. As an alternative, you could have someone else do the research and supply you with the list of ten words. If you're working with another writer, you can each research ten words and exchange lists. The bottom line, regardless of the research method you use, is that you want to have a list of at least ten new and interesting words.

2. Using no other resources except the words and your own imagination, create logical, but whimsical definition.

HERE'S WHAT THIS WORKOUT WILL DO FOR YOU

The benefits of this workout are similar to Workout 1C. In the previous workout, you probably began with a thought in your own mind of which words you wanted to use or which relationship you would exploit. In this workout, you're presumably starting with nothing but a strange-sounding word. It puts more of a burden on your creativity. The results may or may not be as funny, but the workout is worthwhile.

HERE ARE SOME EXAMPLES

prunella: a specialized type of umbrella that is used only in the unlikely event that it rains prune juice.

★   ★   ★   ★   ★

sprent: what a drunk claims he did with all his money.

★   ★   ★   ★   ★

stibiated: the logical conclusion one comes to when there are no doughnuts left in the box, and a lad named "Stibby" is the only one with powdered sugar around his mouth.

Actually, "prunella" is a disorder of the jaws or throat; "sprent" is the obsolete past tense and past participle of the verb "spreng"; and "stibiated" means to be impregnated with antimony, which is a silvery-white, metallic chemical substance.

= WORKOUT 2E =
"Fun With Puns"

We've had some fun with words in this chapter. This last workout will give us a chance to do some research and see how past masters have played with words.

Puns have been maligned as the lowest from of humor. They aren't. They can be and often are, but so are other bad jokes. A good pun can be a funny joke and a fascinating use of language. Oscar Levant said, "A pun is the lowest form of humor when you don't think of it first."

HERE'S WHAT YOU DO FOR THIS WORKOUT

1. Compile a list of ten puns, from your memory, from your reading, from dedicated research, or wherever.

2. Commit your list to paper and study and analyze the clever use of language in the pun.

HERE'S WHAT THIS WORKOUT WILL DO FOR YOU

In searching for puns you like, you'll gain an appreciation of how language can be used in comedy. You'll see different ways to create puns, and how you, as a writer, can use language cleverly.

HERE ARE SOME EXAMPLES

One wit in England claimed that he could ad-lib a pun on any subject. Someone shouted out, "The King." He replied, "The King, Sir, is not a subject."

★　★　★　★　★

Then there's one about a man who accidentally swallowed some varnish. It killed him, but they say he had a fine finish.

★　★　★　★　★

Then there was the man who complained to his wife that the coffee tasted like mud. She said, "Of course it does; it was ground this morning."

= WORKOUT 2F =
"One Person's Idiom Is Another Person's Straight-Line"

Words often work in teams, and when they do they sometimes have a different meaning than they would individually. For instance, "Get on the ball" has nothing to do with climbing onto a ball. It's a phrase that means to improve your performance.

Phrases often have literal meanings that are different from their idiomatic meanings, and as a comedy writer, you can use either meaning or both of them. To illustrate, notice how the meaning changes as you read this following gag:

> "You know, I'm not drinking anymore. Of course, I'm not drinking any less, either."

But the joke doesn't necessarily have to be based on double entendre. Often the meaning of the cliché lends itself to comedy. In this workout, you will analyze and pull apart phrases to find the fun that's hidden in them.

HERE'S WHAT YOU DO FOR THIS WORKOUT

Make a list of at least 20 common phrases, such as:

> "Till death do us part"/"For better or for worse"/"Hitting 50" (*or whatever age*)

HERE'S WHAT THIS WORKOUT WILL DO FOR YOU

This workout has double-barreled rewards. It teaches you to analyze groups of words for the comedy inherent in them, and it gives you practice in pulling apart an idiomatic expression word by word. It also helps you develop a sharper ear for the language.

HERE ARE SOME EXAMPLES

"I'm not too crazy about that wedding vow, 'For better or for worse.' I much prefer 'For better or forget it.'"

★   ★   ★   ★   ★

"I don't plan to be buried in the same cemetery plot with my wife. No sir, our wedding vow said 'Till death do us part,' and I'm holding her to that."

★   ★   ★   ★   ★

"You didn't just hit 50, man. You beat the hell out of it."

A WORD BEFORE YOU START

You can see from these examples that there are many ways to play with the wording of a phrase. In the first example, the preposition, "for," became the first syllable of "forget." The second example applies a literal meaning to the phrase, "Till death do us part," changing it from a loving vow to a loophole. The third exaggerates the literal meaning of "hit" and creates a funny image. Experiment. Find new meanings and have fun with this workout.

Chapter Three

WORKING WITH CAPTIONS

I once worked for a client who asked if I had done any jokes about a particular item that appeared in that morning's newspaper. I confessed I hadn't, and the client was annoyed. He had done a press conference earlier in the day, and one of the reporters asked about that particular topic. The comic had no quotable reply.

I said, "I didn't realize you wanted jokes about that."

He said, "I want to have something to say about everything that happens."

That's quite an assignment for a comedy writer. I'm not sure I could afford the expense of that many typewriter ribbons. But that is the humorist's goal in life—to have a comment ready on practically anything.

Much verbal humor is commentary. It's making a statement about something—an event, a person, a happening.

If you review the joke examples in Workout 1A (and it might be a good idea to do that right now—read them over quickly before continuing), you'll see that they follow a particular form. They make a factual statement, then they comment on it. Some one-liners may simply be the comment, because the statement either has been made previously or is assumed. The comment is like a caption on a factual statement.

Most of us are familiar with captions. We see them done on the Johnny Carson show periodically. We've seen books with comic captions applied to paintings, statues, and photographs of all kinds. Most cartoons, of course, are drawings with captions.

The photograph, drawings, or whatever is the set-up, and the caption is the punchline. Captioning is an easy form of joke writing because the straight-line is furnished for us. We don't have to begin writing from scratch; we have the photo or the drawing as our starting point. We merely have to funny it up.

Many one-liners are exactly the same, except that we have to provide both the set-up and the punchline. The writing of jokes or one-liners seems a bit easier if we remember that the factual statement is the setup. Then we simply have to find a caption for it—a punchline that makes it funny.

If you can caption a photograph or a cartoon, you can caption a statement. That's writing jokes.

= WORKOUT 3A =

"A Picture Is Worth a Thousand Punchlines"

A picture is supposed to be worth a thousand words. That's probably because a photograph can be very eloquently understated. It allows you—the viewer—to do the talking. You can interpret that picture any way you like.

As we saw with words and with phrases, images can have a real and an imagined interpretation. In fact, several real interpretations may be possible. Is the person in the photograph going up or coming down the ladder?

The humorist can assign a new and different meaning to any action in a picture. We see a boxer kneeling on the canvas. Obviously, he has been knocked down by his opponent. To the comedy writer, though, he may simply be looking for a contact lens. Or he might be praying. He can be doing anything the inventive mind of the writer wants him to be doing.

In this workout you'll study photographs for hidden or different meanings and create a caption that explains your idea of what is going on.

HERE'S WHAT YOU DO FOR THIS WORKOUT

1. Find and collect 25 interesting photographs. Ideally, these should all be of one particular type: old movie photos, horror movie photos, baby pictures, sports photographs, or any theme you prefer.

They can be actual photographs, or clippings from magazines or newspapers. Get them anywhere you can find them.

2. Write a funny caption for each photograph.

HERE'S WHAT THIS WORKOUT WILL DO FOR YOU

This is good training in looking beyond the obvious. You see the action before you, and the action is generally fairly obvious. However, in order to generate humor, you might have to see something in the photo that isn't obvious. At least, it isn't obvious until you point it out to the viewer.

For instance, your photograph might show someone yawning. But your caption may suggest that the person is not yawning, but singing, or screaming, or bobbing for watermelons, or anything else that requires opening the mouth that wide.

This workout is good training, too, in phrasing your caption in a clever, unique way—a way that tells the story you want to tell the viewer clearly, concisely, and with maximum humor.

HERE ARE SOME EXAMPLES

In captioning photos, it's usually best to come up with an idea that assigns a completely new meaning to the action in the photograph. You may be able to get a joke from the action as it exists, but inventiveness usually adds to the humor. Let me illustrate.

Let's assume you're going with a photograph from a horror movie that shows a monster strangling a man. He has a garrote around his victim's throat and is pulling with all his strength.

One caption might say, "Please. Igor, loosen it a little bit so I can cry out for help." That's fine, but it is leaving the action in the photograph exactly the way it was intended—the monster is choking his victim.

★   ★   ★   ★   ★

Another caption might say, "Thank you, Igor, but I think I'll get someone else to help me with my bow tie." Now the action in the scene changes. The monster is not murdering the victim, he's merely helping him with the ever troublesome tying of a bow tie. It's funnier now. In trying to be friendly and helpful, he's got the hapless gentleman gasping for air.

★   ★   ★   ★   ★

Another caption may say, "This may feel a little uncomfortable at first, but many of our clients have lost a lot of weight with this diet." Now the monster is tying a cord around the client's neck not to strangle him, but to help him lose weight.

A WORD BEFORE YOU START

Study the photographs that you've selected and search out other meanings that they might have. The meanings can be subtle or they can be bizarre, but they should be different from the real action of the photo. Then try to find a short caption that tells "your" story to the viewer—clearly and humorously.

Finding the photographs should be fun and making them funny should be, too.

= WORKOUT 3B =
"Pen and Ink Patter"

Pen and ink is mightier than the photograph. At least it's mightier in that it is more versatile. You can only photograph what actually exists; you can draw anything your mind can imagine. Therefore, you can see things in cartoons that you can't in photos.

For example, with pen and ink you can show a person flattened out after being rolled over by a steamroller. We all accept that. The poor victim is only a half inch high, but everything else is in perfect proportion. The belt is still around the middle of the torso, the tie is still on, and so on. Naturally, a photograph of such a tragedy wouldn't look like that. That's the magic of cartooning.

In the previous workout you captioned actual photos; in this one, you'll caption cartoons. The straight line you have to work with—the drawing—can be wackier, more bizarre.

HERE'S WHAT YOU DO FOR THIS WORKOUT

1. Collect 25 cartoons that have drawings that you feel lend themselves to good comedy. Discard the caption that is on them.

If you prefer, you could have someone else collect interesting cartoons for you and discard the captions before you see them. That way your humor won't be influenced by the original creators' jokes.

You could also work with another writer, collect cartoons, discard the captions, and exchange them.

Whatever method you select, have at least 25 captionless cartoons at your disposal.

2. Write new captions for each cartoon.

HERE'S WHAT THIS WORKOUT WILL DO FOR YOU

The value of this workout is the same as for Workout 3A, with the added benefit that you learn to see things with a whimsical eye. You will learn from the cartoonists' drawings that a thing doesn't have to be real or even possible for it to exist in your mind. Artists can draw anything that their minds can visualize. Once they draw it, other minds can visualize it, too.

This phenomenon is true of ideas, also. Artists and writers are not limited by reality. We are all free to create a new reality—the reality of our imagination.

HERE ARE SOME EXAMPLES

In this workout, you needn't search for hidden meanings. The cartoonists have done that for you. You're searching for a logical reason for their craziness.

For example, suppose your cartoon shows a cavalry officer speaking with an Indian Chief who is surrounded by hundreds of his warriors. The cavalry officer has literally hundreds of arrows sticking out of him, from all over his body. He looks like a porcupine. You don't need to change the characters. They can remain an officer talking to an Indian Chief. What you must search for is the reason why the officer has been riddled with arrows.

Here are a few possibilities:

"I apologize, Chief. I was always led to believe that 'How' was a *friendly* Indian greeting."

★　　★　　★　　★　　★

"Chief, I'm going to take this to mean that you weren't happy with the wording of the Peace Treaty."

★　　★　　★　　★　　★

"General Custer warned me that you were a sneaky little %#@$#&."

A WORD BEFORE YOU START

Some of the drawings you find may be so bizarre and unrealistic that it's hard to find any logic for them. However, the original artists saw some reason to draw them, and with some effort you can find a variation on that reasoning.

It's good comedy writing practice, so have fun with this workout.

= WORKOUT 3C =
"Inanimate Playhouse"

Everything you see tells a story. The photograph is real action, the cartoon is imaginary action, now we'll see that even inanimate objects can take action—at least in the mind.

In this workout, you'll provide the image, the imagination, and the caption.

HERE'S WHAT YOU DO FOR THIS WORKOUT

1. Create and stage a scene that you will caption. Limit yourself to just one area—anything related to:

   a. Food
   b. Stationery or office supplies
   c. Shoes and socks
   d. Handyman's tools
   e. Letters of the alphabet

In creating and staging your scene, be as inventive as you want, but use only items from the area you selected. Food can be milk cartons, fruit, pretzels, snacks, soft drinks, whatever. Office supplies can be paper clips, staplers, rulers, pens, pencils, paper, and so on. Shoes may be ladies' shoes or men's shoes, athletic footwear, loafers, boots, or baby shoes—anything people put on their feet. Handyman's tools can range from screwdrivers and hammers all the way up to electric power tools. Letters of the alphabet can be typewritten, handwritten, ornate, scribbled—any type of letter at all.

The scene that you create should give some life to these objects—a life that your caption (step 2) will explain.

2. Caption the scene that you have just created.

HERE'S WHAT THIS WORKOUT WILL DO FOR YOU

This workout will give you some practice in assigning different meanings, purposes, and intents to ordinary, inanimate objects. It will train your imagination to put some life into everything. It will train you to see things for what they are, and also for what they might be.

HERE ARE SOME EXAMPLES

Here are some sample cartoons that I created using food:

1. In this scene I set up two soft pretzels. One is plain; the other is covered with mustard. The caption reads:

"You're a nice girl, Mabel, but I think you use too much make-up."

★　　★　　★　　★　　★

2. A plum is pictured next to a peach. The caption reads:

"The next time you expect to kiss me goodnight, Orville, you'd better shave first."

★　　★　　★　　★　　★

3. A can of sardines lies open. One solitary sardine is lying beside the can. The caption reads:

"Why is it always me that has to wait for the next elevator?"

A WORD BEFORE YOU START

It's hard to summarize this workout because it can go in any direction. However, it's good all around practice for creating, visualizing, and thinking funny.

Have fun working at it.

= WORKOUT 3D =
"Caption Your Own"

For this workout, we're removing all restrictions on your imagination and inventiveness. You're free to go hog wild.

You're going to create your own workout. It's just like a place where you make your own sundaes: you can add your favorite flavor or ice cream, your own toppings, and as much whipped cream as you like.

In fact, this is so free-wheeling, I'll even dispense with the normal format.

HERE'S WHAT YOU DO FOR THIS WORKOUT

Come up with your own zany idea of something—anything—that you can caption. Whatever you come up with, do at least ten of them.

And, as always, have fun with it.

Chapter Four

WORKING WITH RELATIONSHIPS

Here are four jokes that I've researched. They are different jokes from several comedians on varying subjects. On the surface they don't appear alike at all. Study them, though, and see if you can discover some similarity among them.

"Have I got a mother-in-law! She's so neat she tries to put paper under the cuckoo clock."

—Henny Youngman

★ ★ ★ ★ ★

"This afternoon my wife told me she gave me the best years of her life. What worries me now is what's coming up."

—Rodney Dangerfield

★ ★ ★ ★ ★

"I recently bought a dozen golf balls and the salesman asked me if he should wrap them up. I said, 'No, I'll drive them home.' "

—Jack Carter

★ ★ ★ ★ ★

"Sex is a beautiful thing between two people. Between five it's fantastic."

—Woody Allen

★ ★ ★ ★ ★

"I have a scheme for stopping war. It's this . . . no nation is allowed to enter a war till they have paid for the last one."

—Will Rogers

What all of the gags have in common, and what most gags have in common, is that they take one basic premise and relate it to another idea. To illustrate: Henny Youngman's basic idea was how neat his mother-in-law was, so he related it to putting paper under anything that could cause a mess. He exaggerated it to the point where she put the paper under something that couldn't cause a mess—the bird in the cuckoo clock.

Dangerfield's primary topic was the years his wife had given him. He related them to the upcoming years.

Jack Carter was talking about golf balls. He related them to driving, and then did a play on the word "drive," relating to both hitting a golf ball and steering a car.

Woody Allen used a device that we'll have some workouts on later (working with alternate meanings). He took a phrase that emphasized the word "between" and switched that emphasis to the word "two." He related sex between two to sex among five.

Will Rogers related war to paying for war.

Now analyze the jokes that you selected in Workout 1A. You will probably find that most of them are based on the interrelationship of two ideas.

This relationship is the basis for the most humor. The comedian states the basic premise, then compares it to another idea. This second idea is often similar to the first, but it can also be opposite. It's related by being so unrelated—the same way a word can have synonyms and antonyms. Sometimes the second idea has no connection with the original premise at all: it's a complete nonsequitur. As an example:

"It's better to have loved and lost than to get your lip caught under a manhole cover."

With these types of jokes, the second idea is often a mini-joke in itself. It's a funny sounding or image-producing phrase, that would almost stand alone. For example, you could put a completely different premise before this example and have a new joke that works just as well.

"There is nothing worse than a woman scorned except maybe a woman who gets her lip caught under a manhole cover."

There are three basic types of relationships—similar, opposite, and unrelated. Think of the word association test that psychologists give. The doctor offers a word and the patient is supposed to respond with the first word that comes to mind.

The doctor could say "black"; the patient might respond "ink." That would be a similar response. However, the doctor could say "black"; the patient might say "white." That's a logical but opposite relationship. Or the doctor could say "black" and the patient could respond "Pee Wee Herman's undershirt." That obviously is a non-related response. It probably means the patient's either crazy or a comedy writer.

Exploring these relationships is the first step in writing comedy. To get a joke on paper, you usually begin with your basic premise—what you want to talk about—and something that it's related to. Once you have those items you can begin to search for the phrasing, the wording, the expressions that you'll use to get your idea across.

More importantly, though, learning to discover, uncover, and create these relationships—similar, dissimilar, or unrelated—give you a broader base for your comedy. It gives you more ideas to select from, and it gives more variety to your comedy.

You're like an artist. The more colors on your palette, the more shading, detail, and depth you can add to your painting.

The following workouts will help you practise finding the relationships that will aid in your comedy writing.

= WORKOUT 4A =
"That Goes With This"

This workout will be practice in searching out *similar* ideas to relate to your basic premise. Below are the two basic ideas that you will be working on:

1. Mikhail Gorbachev visiting New York City in December of 1988. He travelled around the city extensively, visiting many tourist attractions and attending official meetings. He travelled, though, in a motorcade of 49 cars. That's your premise—the size of that motorcade.

★　　★　　★　　★　　★

2. Some years ago Queen Elizabeth II visited California and was scheduled to visit then President Reagan's Santa Barbara ranch and then enjoy some horseback riding with the President. However, heavy rains threatened to cancel the riding.

Your premise is this: The Queen and the President would ride despite the rains and wet conditions.

HERE'S WHAT YOU DO FOR THIS WORKOUT

1. List 15 things that might be associated with a motorcade of 49 cars.
2. List 15 ways that might allow the Queen and the President to ride in wet conditions. For instance, what kind of horse would be safe in that weather, or how could they doctor the horse or the equipment to ride safely in the rain?
3. Using items from the lists that you compile, write five jokes on the Gorbachev motorcade, and five jokes on the horseback riding in the rain.

HERE'S WHAT THIS WORKOUT WILL DO FOR YOU

You'll learn how some mental effort helps you to uncover relationships. At first, it seems impossible to think of 15 things related to a motorcade, but you may surprise yourself.

More importantly, you'll learn that once you have these relationships established, the joke writing becomes easier. The ideas present jokes to your mind.

HERE ARE SOME EXAMPLES

Here are a few of the items that I dreamed up about the motorcade, along with some of the jokes that they inspired:

a funeral procession　　　　　a pile-up

a parade　　　　　　　　　　a game of follow-the-leader

a traffic jam

"Gorbachev's a man who leaves nothing to chance. He carries his own funeral procession with him when he travels."

★　　★　　★　　★　　★

"Talk about bringing coals to Newcastle. Here's a man who brings his own traffic jam to New York City."

★   ★   ★   ★   ★

"I hope he brought along good drivers. Can you imagine how long it would take to file an accident report involving 49 cars?"

Here are some of the ideas that relate to riding a horse in wet conditions, along with the resulting jokes:

> get a horse with webbed feet
>
> get a horse that treads water
>
> hook an outboard motor to the horse
>
> get a horse with oars
>
> get a horse that is at home in the water

"They've decided that the Queen is going to go riding despite the weather. They've finally come up with a horse that has webbed feet."

★   ★   ★   ★   ★

"The Queen is going to go riding with the President. They got the saddles on the horses with no problem. The most difficult part was keeping the horses still while they hooked up the outboard motors."

★   ★   ★   ★   ★

"The Queen and the President are going to go riding today. The President shouldn't have any trouble, but it'll be hard for the Queen to row while sitting side-saddle."

★   ★   ★   ★   ★

"The President rode his regular horse, while the Queen rode 'Shamu, the Killer Stallion.' "

A WORD BEFORE YOU START

You can see that each relationship practically leads you directly to its own joke. The wording and the exposition of the punchline might need some fine-tuning, but once you get the idea, the humor is there.

You'll discover that you're writing jokes where you didn't think you could before. Instead of going right to the joke, you go for the relationship first. That makes the writing easier.

Have fun with this exercise.

= WORKOUT 4B =
"This Doesn't Go With That"

This workout will be practice in uncovering _dissimilar_ relationships—those that relate to your premise by being practically opposite.

Use the same two premises that you used in Workout 4A.

HERE'S WHAT YOU DO FOR THIS WORKOUT

1. List 15 ideas or relationships that you _would not_ associate with a 49-car motorcade.

2. List 15 reasons why the Queen and the President could not ride in the wet conditions. For example, what type of horse or equipment wouldn't be safe in rainy, wet weather.

3. Using items from the lists that you compile, write five jokes on the Gorbachev motorcade, and five jokes on the horseback riding in the rain.

HERE'S WHAT THIS WORKOUT WILL DO FOR YOU

You'll see a whole new approach to establishing relationships. Even though these relationships are opposite, once the connection is made the interrelationship is valid. These connections lead just as easily to jokes.

This new dimension will add variety to your writing. The same principles apply, but your humor takes on a slightly different character. When you do a lot of writing, those nuances are important to give your humor variety and depth.

You'll learn from this workout, too, that by approaching your topic from a different direction you expand the topic. You open up new ideas and should produce more material.

HERE ARE SOME EXAMPLES

Here are a few items I listed as not consistent with 49 cars driven as a unit, and some of the jokes that resulted:

> a getaway car
>
> belonging to the auto club
>
> finding a parking space
>
> being inconspicuous
>
> gassing up

"It's the first time I ever felt sorry for Gorbachev. Can you imagine driving around New York looking for 49 parking spaces?"

★　　★　　★　　★　　★

"Imagine a 49-car motorcade. Boy, I'd hate to get his monthly bill from the Auto Club."

★　　★　　★　　★　　★

"When the motorcade pulled into a corner gas station, the owner got on the phone to his wife and said, 'Tell Jimmy and Sue to start packing, Mom. The kids are going to college after all.'"

Here are some of the ideas that I didn't feel were consistent with wet horseback riding, and some of the jokes that grew from them.

a horse that can't swim

a horse that's afraid of water

a horse that doesn't have non-skid hoofs

a horse that leaks

a horse that stalls in wet weather

"The horse that the Queen had refused to go out in the wet conditions. They should have known better than to get a horse who had just seen the movie, *Jaws, Part 2*."

★   ★   ★   ★   ★

"The Queen's horse reared up when they got out on the trail. He was spooked by a passing school of tuna."

★   ★   ★   ★   ★

"The Queen almost drowned during the ride. Unfortunately, they got her a horse who only knew how to float on his back."

A WORD BEFORE YOU START

You can see that these jokes fit with the basic premise just as well as the previous jokes, though they were arrived at from a different angle. It's like having two routes to get to your destination. Both of them get you there, but they add a little variety and some options.

Have fun with this workout.

= WORKOUT 4C =
"That Makes Absolutely No Sense at All"

This workout provides practice in using the *non sequitur* type of relationship. This device can quickly become cloying if used too much, especially in the same routine, but it's very effective when used sparingly. It's a zany type of humor, and it adds flavor and variety to your writing.

HERE'S WHAT YOU DO FOR THIS WORKOUT

1. Compile a list of 15 aphorisms—short proverbs that are almost clichés. In a previous example, I used a variation on "It's better to have loved and lost than never to have loved at all."

These don't have to be witty. In fact, it's better if they aren't. They just have to be recognizable.

2. Select ten aphorisms from you list, and turn them into jokes by changing the ending to something completely ridiculous that is not associated with the first part of the sentence. You may change the original ending or simply add on to it.

HERE'S WHAT THIS WORKOUT WILL DO FOR YOU

You'll create some bizarre, wacky sayings. This will add a little craziness to your humor that will provide a welcome change of pace.

HERE ARE SOME EXAMPLES

Here are a few of the jokes that I concocted from sayings that you'll recognize:

"Look before you leap—especially if you have a neighbor whose hobby is siphoning swimming pools."

★　　★　　★　　★　　★

"Always a bridesmaid, never a bride. Strange kind of a hobby for a lumberjack to have."

★　　★　　★　　★　　★

"Haste makes waste. And waste makes great leftovers that you can serve whenever the in-laws come to visit."

A WORD BEFORE YOU START

This workout is a stimulator. It has no rules or regulations. It only promotes creativity, and gets your mind thinking in unorthodox ways.

Sometimes we get hung up on "correct" ways of doing things and traditional approaches. This should jar you out of that rut.

Have fun with it.

= WORKOUT 4D =
"What Can You Say About So-and-So?"

This is a combination workout. You can use any of the techniques that you learned in Workout 4A, 4B, and 4C. Your basic focus in this workout will be a familiar personality.

HERE'S WHAT YOU DO FOR THIS WORKOUT

1. Make a list of five celebrities from any field—sports, movies, politics, or whatever—who are noted for a particular characteristic. For instance, Zsa Zsa Gabor is noted for her frequent marriages, George Burns for his age, Dolly Parton . . . well, you get the idea.

2. Compile a list of five relationships having to do with each celebrity's characteristics.

3. Write one joke about each celebrity you listed using one of the relationships that you noted.

HERE'S WHAT THIS WORKOUT WILL DO FOR YOU

This exercise gives you your choice of using any of the relationships that we mentioned—similar, opposite, or non sequitur. It's practice in becoming aware of the options that are available to you in comedy writing, exploring all of them, and selecting the one you'll use for a particular joke.

This exercise will show you that the more options you have to choose from in your writing, the better your writing will be.

HERE ARE SOME EXAMPLES

I've selected Sammy Davis as an example. Sammy is noted for the expensive gold rings, necklaces, and other baubles that he wears.

My list of relationships would be:

> great wealth
>
> jewelry store
>
> King Tut
>
> King Midas
>
> gold fillings

From that preparation, I created this joke:

> "I met and shook hands with Sammy Davis the other day. When I did, I had more money in my hand than I had in my wallet."

A WORD BEFORE YOU START

This workout is similar to the previous ones, except that it's fun working with celebrities. Have fun with it.

Chapter Five

WORKING WITH IMAGERY

Two men were playing golf at the club one day. One gentleman was winning easily. Not only was he winning, but he was enjoying his victory, rubbing it in with sarcastic asides. The loser didn't accept the defeat or the ignominy graciously; but he did endure them silently.

In the clubhouse locker room, they settled the financial part of the defeat. Then as the loser dressed, the winner noticed he was a priest. He put on the Roman collar.

Now the victor was embarrassed. He said, "I'm sorry. I had no idea you were a priest."

The clergyman said, "Yes, I am. Bring your parents around to the church sometime and I'll marry them."

The good Father called his antagonist a bastard without saying it—but by creating a vivid word picture. That's using imagery!

When I was head-writer for a comedy-variety show, the star of the show often told me to have the writers "hide the joke a little more." That means to disguise the punchline rather than make it a statement.

In our example above, the priest could have paid off the debt and said, "Here's your money, you bastard." That's not a joke. When he politely *implies* that his opponent's parents never married, thus calling him a bastard, it's funny. It's different. It's clever. That's disguising the punchline.

One way to hide the punchline is to say something by not really saying it. Imply it, like the priest did. Use a colorful image that gets your idea across, but doesn't really *say* it.

When you tell someone you'll get two Boy Scouts to help him across the street, you're saying he's old.

When you ask someone to hold your wallet but warn that you've counted the money, you're implying that that person is a thief.

When you tell someone to stand up when he's talking to you, and he is standing, you're saying he's short. You're saying all these things without really saying them.

There are several reasons why imagery helps your humor.

First, it can make your punchline more interesting, more colorful, and more graphic. Poets use images for that reason all the time. When we hear that the fog "creeps in on little cat feet," we can almost see it moving into the city, cautiously yet deliberately. We see in our mind the speed at which it moves.

Humor is best when it's most graphic. A good image can produce a powerful picture in the listener's mind. That enhances the comedy.

Second, a good joke has a certain rhythm to it. It's a seat-of-the-pants kind of rhythm with few rules and regulations, but the comic feels when it's right and when it's wrong. The use of imagery can sometimes stretch the punchline out to a more manageable number of syllables. It can add a lilt to the joke that helps comedy timing.

In our golf game example above, the word "bastard" was too direct. It allowed no room for the joke to fall out smoothly. It came out harsh and rude. The image wording, though, came out softer. It allowed the priest to speak delicately, politely, yet offer the same insult.

Third, imagery challenges the listener. It makes the audience think. Probably, when you read the story that opened this chapter you were puzzled. It made no sense to you, until you realized what the statement meant. Then you saw the humor of it. That made you a part of the story. You chuckled or at least smiled inwardly as a reward to yourself. You solved the puzzle. You figured out the punchline.

That's a big part of humor. The audience likes to have something left to the imagination. They want to do part of the work. The ideal joke is one that hides just enough of the punchline to make the audience have to figure it out, but they need to be able to figure it out quickly enough so that the premise isn't destroyed. Obviously, there's no reward for a nightclub comedian in telling jokes that the audience will understand and finally laugh at as they're driving home.

Imagery can hide the punchline, and still be clear enough so the listeners catch on quickly enough to enjoy it.

Fourth, saying the punchline without really saying it adds some surprise, and surprise is a major part of comedy. The payload is less of a direct statement. It's less abrupt. The audience might be expecting a direct statement, but they don't hear it. Then they realize that they really did hear it, but it was disguised, hidden. That's comedy.

W. C. Fields, who knew a little bit about humor, said that comedy is when you expect something to break, but it only bends.

In the following workouts, you'll practice substituting an alternate meaning or a visual image for some statement or idea. The work may be challenging, but it will pay hefty dividends in your comedy writing.

= WORKOUT 5A =
"Say It With Pictures"

Most success depends on elbow grease, burning the midnight oil, and cracking the books. Translated that means hard work, late hours, and study. But the sentence never said those things. It didn't have to. The images said them more graphically and more colorfully.

"Elbow grease" is only one cliché phrase that denotes effort. There are others. "Break a sweat," "Lift that barge and tote that bale," "Keep your nose to the grindstone," and "Put your shoulder to the wheel," are other common symbols for dedicated labor. There are non-cliché symbols, too. Those are the ones that inventive minds create.

These can be used effectively in writing comedy. I remember my mother once cheering up a friend who was having some bad luck. My Mom said, "Don't worry, Agnes. Your ship will come in." Agnes replied, "Mary, by the time my ship comes in, my pier will have collapsed."

This workout will be practice in searching out symbols or images for common, ordinary words and ideas. You'll recall everyday expressions that you can use, and you'll also create some new ones.

HERE'S WHAT YOU DO FOR THIS WORKOUT

1. List ten images or symbols for each of the following words:

> Red
>
> Blue
>
> Yellow
>
> Green
>
> Purple

2. List ten images or symbols for each of the following ideas:

> Short
>
> Tall
>
> Muscular
>
> Sensual
>
> Strong

3. List ten images or symbols for each of the following ideas:

> Lucky
>
> Stingy
>
> Sexy
>
> Shy
>
> Arrogant

HERE'S WHAT THIS WORKOUT WILL DO FOR YOU

From this workout you'll learn to see beyond the word or the basic idea. You'll learn to see a graphic, living embodiment of it. Work is no longer just a four-letter word; it becomes a person leaning into something with all of his or her might—putting "elbow grease" into the project. You can almost feel the person sweating as the slaves did when they had to push heavy stone wheels up a hill—putting their shoulder to the wheel.

This skill will help your comedy writing in at least two ways. First, it can give you more colorful gags. Second, it gives you more graphic images to select from in creating your joke relationships.

HERE ARE SOME EXAMPLES

I've chosen colors for my illustration. Following is a list of 20 symbols that imply the color "white."

1. Snow flurries or blizzard	11. Polar bear
2. Purity	12. Caucasian
3. Good Humor truck	13. Flour
4. Movie screen	14. Sugar
5. Field of lilies	15. Cake frosting
6. Ku Klux Klan uniform (white sheets)	16. Milk
7. Inside of a Ping-Pong ball	17. Vanilla
8. Bride	18. The Pope
9. Nurse	19. Ghost
10. Swan	20. Blank sheet of paper

A WORD BEFORE YOU START

There are no jokes in this workout, but there is much joke potential. This is some of the research that you need to do in order to find the second half of a joke.

For instance, if you're at a formal party where all the men are dressed in traditional black tuxedoes, and then one person comes in wearing an all white tux with white shirt, white tie and cummerbund, and white shoes and socks, that guy is your joke premise. The 20 items above are the images or symbols that you might liken his costume to. There are jokes hidden in that list somewhere.

The next workout will help you see the connection. But first put a little mental "elbow grease" into this workout, and have fun with it.

= WORKOUT 5B =
"Say It With Funny Pictures"

This workout will use the research you did in Workout 5A to create comedy.

HERE'S WHAT YOU DO FOR THIS WORKOUT

1. Create a comedy premise for each of the 15 different items you worked on in Workout 5A. For the color section, you might have a friend of yours wearing a strikingly red sweater or garish purple socks. In the second part, you might comment on how muscular a certain football player is. In the last section you might be doing lines about the luck you had in Vegas or how sexy your new girlfriend is.

2. Using the symbols that you created for each item, do at least two jokes on each comedy premise.

Write 30 jokes altogether, two each on the 15 separate topics.

HERE'S WHAT THIS WORKOUT WILL DO FOR YOU

This workout will teach you to convert the imagery that you create into usable comedy lines.

HERE ARE SOME EXAMPLES

Using my examples from Workout 5A, I've created the comedy premise (borrowed from Phyllis Diller) of a mother-in-law who is very large. I have her wearing a white dress. You could work this same premise, incidentally, with other colors, also. "When she wore a green dress" . . . "When she wore a yellow dress" . . . and so on.

Here are my lines about Phyllis Diller's mother-in-law, Moby Dick:

"This woman is huge. When she wears a white dress we show home movies on her."

★　　★　　★　　★　　★

"She was always large. When she came down the aisle as a bride, 14 guests were overcome with snow blindness."

★　　★　　★　　★　　★

"In that white bride's gown she looked like a Good Humor truck"

★　　★　　★　　★　　★

". . . with the tailgate down."

I also did some similar lines many years ago for a black comedian. These came out about the time the movie *Lawrence of Arabia* was playing in the first-run theatres.

"I wouldn't go see that movie *Lawrence of Arabia*. I can't enjoy a movie that has that many people running around in white sheets."

★　　★　　★　　★　　★

". . . I get nervous if I see two or three Good Humor men hanging around together."

Here's an example of this same comedian using imagery with the color black:

"I firmly believe what my people are saying, that 'black is beautiful.' So I painted my house black, inside and out. I bought black furniture. I bought black clothing for me, my wife, and my children. First thing I lost was my bowling ball."

A WORD BEFORE YOU START

You can sense how the joke almost flowed out of the research. By doing the advance work, figuring out some references and symbols, the second part of the joke fell into place.

By now you'll probably be able to sense that a joke could be written about Moby Dick wearing white, using any one of the 20 images that I listed in Workout 5A.

When the preparatory work is done well, the writing becomes easier and faster, and you should be able to write more and better jokes.

See if this workout doesn't prove that to be true. Have fun with it.

= WORKOUT 5C =
"The Bobsled Man's Bottom"

This workout is more complex, more difficult, and more challenging. It's also harder to explain. For that reason, I'm going to give the example now so it will be easier for you to understand how it works.

Jack Benny used colorful imagery to explain comedically how blue his eyes were. He said:

> "My eyes are as blue as the bottom of the fourth man on a three-man bobsled team."

You'll notice how he used a few ideas to convey his imagery. The listener has to visualize that the fourth man doesn't fit on a three-man bobsled, therefore his bottom would hang over. It would hang over onto snow. Snow is cold, and cold turns your skin blue.

It's a long way to go, but the very complexity of it is funny, and the image is funny.

HERE'S WHAT YOU DO FOR THIS WORKOUT

Select two examples from each of the three sections in Workout 5A and try to construct visual images that roughly follow the form of Jack Benny's joke.

HERE'S WHAT THIS WORKOUT WILL DO FOR YOU

This workout stretches your imagination. It flexes the comedic muscles. It is admittedly difficult, but that's good. It should strengthen your creativity.

Have fun with it.

= WORKOUT 5D =
"Say It By Not Saying It"

Someone once explained that part of the charm of comedy is that it says something people are thinking, but says it in a way they would never have thought of.

That's part of the purpose of this series of workouts—to learn to state ordinary ideas in an extraordinary way.

This workout will be good practice in converting the pedestrian to the unique.

HERE'S WHAT YOU DO FOR THIS WORKOUT

1. Compile a list of 20 cliché metaphors or similes, like these:

"Drunk as a skunk"   "Cold as ice"   "He swore like a sailor"

"Cool as a cucumber"   "A little devil"

2. Rewrite the saying. Using the same basic premise, restate the cliché using funnier symbolism. In other words, say it by not saying it. Say "sailor" by implying it. Rewrite at least 10 of your original list of 20.

HERE'S WHAT THIS WORKOUT WILL DO FOR YOU

This workout will force you to look beyond the obvious. You have to depend on your creativity to turn a trite saying into unique, original language.

It's good practice in going beyond the obvious humor and searching for something just a little bit better, a bit more comedic.

HERE ARE SOME EXAMPLES

"This man could try the patience of a saint."

converted to:

"I'll give you an idea what kind of guy he was. St. Francis of Assisi would have punched him in the mouth."

"The evening dragged."

converted to:

"What a long, boring night. I glanced at my watch at midnight and it only read 8:30."

A WORD BEFORE YOU START

The clichés say a lot. They have a touch of irony in them already. Your rephrasing should say the same thing, but say it with more visual impact. In my examples, you can "see" a saint in sandals and robe so upset with this guy that he decks him. You can "see" a person looking at his timepiece and not believing that it's only 8:30.

You'll come up with better examples. Have fun with this workout.

Chapter Six

WORKING WITH ALTERNATE MEANINGS

The magician holds up a ball and says, "I'm going to place this ball under the gold cup." After making that move, he points to the cup, perhaps taps it a few times. He focuses all eyes on that cup.

Of course, the ball isn't under there at all. He never placed it there; he simply *said* he did. And we believed him. It looked like he put it there, and he *said* he put it there. He seems to be focusing all of his attention on it, so we do, too.

While we're concentrating on the gold cup, the sleight-of-hand artist is hiding the ball in his pocket. That's misdirection.

The performer purposely misled us into thinking he did something with the ball that he didn't; then he focused our attention on the wrong place to distract us. While we're looking at the gold cup, the ball magically appears from behind the magician's elbow.

Words and phrases can do the same thing to us, the audience. Someone says something to us. We're sure we know what it means. Then the performer springs an entirely different translation on us. While we're looking at the gold cup, the true meaning comes from behind the elbow.

My Dad used to spring a riddle on us kids. He'd pose this baseball query: One team gets 16 hits in one inning, but not a man crosses the plate. How? We'd struggle with it. My brothers and I would dream up every conceivable situation, but we could never come up with more than six hits without a man crossing the plate.

Then Dad would give us the answer: The team was the "Birmingham Bloomer Girls." Get it? "Not a *man*" crossed the plate.

We assumed that "not a man crosses the plate" was idiomatic for "not a run scored." Wrong. Dad, in his cornpone jest, meant it literally. When he said "man," he meant "man."

Another joke I read as a youngster illustrates the point further. The joke question asked, "Can you tell me how long cows should be milked?" The answer was, "The same as short cows."

Most of us would group the words "how long" together. We think the sentence is asking what length of time cows should be milked. The narrator, though, is grouping the two words, "long cows," together. Obviously, that changes the question to "by what method should long cows be milked as opposed to short cows?"

You've all heard the standard joke reply to the question, "How do I get to Carnegie Hall?" "Practise, practise." Again, the question has an assumed meaning. That is: Can you give me directions on how to get from where I am now to Carnegie Hall? But there are hidden meanings in the phrasing, too. One of them is: How do I get to become a good enough performer to merit an appearance at the prestigious Carnegie Hall?

What's interesting is that none of these phrases is forced or unnatural. Each one is a well-phrased, grammatically correct, easily understood sentence. And the meaning is obvious—we think. However, each has another meaning—a secondary interpretation. Probably, each one has a third and fourth interpretation, too.

Most sentences, no matter how well constructed or how carefully thought out by the author, do have secondary meanings. Take for example, this simple declarative sentence: "I want to go home."

The meaning of that seems obvious. But is it? What is the speaker really saying? You can give three different shadings to that sentence just by saying it with different emphasis.

Try it. Say it three times, each time emphasizing the underlined word. Like this:

I want to go home.

I _want_ to go home.

I want to go _home_.

You can hear the difference.

The first means the speaker is the one who wants to leave. Someone else probably doesn't, but the speaker doesn't care who else goes along. He or she is definitely heading homeward.

The second denotes a strong desire, a goal. There are obstacles. It may not be possible to head home. Who knows? But this person definitely wants to go and may not get there.

The third emphasizes where the speaker is going. Others may want to go to a movie. They may want to stay right where they are. None of that matters. The speaker has only one destination and is ready to fight off all other possibilities.

Sometimes, the alternate meaning might come from the words themselves. For example, this innocent question, "Can you tell me how I can get to Broad and Market streets?" can have at least three different shades of meanings.

The reply to the obvious meaning would be, "Go straight ahead two blocks, then turn right."

However, if you emphasize the first word, "Can," the response might simply be, "Yes."

Emphasize the word, "I," and the answer might be, "The same as everyone else gets there."

We can use these alternate meanings for comedy. How? Groucho Marx showed us with this line from one of his films in which he was on safari:

"Last night I shot a lion in my pajamas. How he got in my pajamas I'll never know."

The joke obviously needs no explanation, but the mechanics of it might. We assume from the first sentence that Groucho was the one wearing the pajamas. He tells us in the next sentence that he wasn't.

Doing these workouts with alternate meanings is good training in looking beyond the obvious. Most sentences have a primary meaning, an interpretation that hits you right between the eyes. The creative writer learns to go further. Looking beyond the obvious—not just with sentences, but with thoughts and ideas—is a major facet of humor.

These workouts will help you to analyze your sentences for hidden meanings. That skill serves a comedy writer well. Much of comedy creating is investigative. You have to pull a topic, an idea, a subject apart before you can write well about it. These workouts are good practice.

The workouts emphasize the element of surprise in humor. The primary meaning is so strong that most people migrate to that one. When the comedian springs a second or third meaning on them, it stuns them. It surprises the audience and produces the laugh.

These workouts should be fun, enlightening, and beneficial.

= WORKOUT 6A =
"But It Could Also Mean"

This workout is practice in searching out the hidden meanings in almost any sentence.

HERE'S WHAT YOU DO FOR THIS WORKOUT

1. Collect at least 20 sentences, declarative or interrogative, and jot them down. The sentences may come from any book, magazine, or newspaper, or they can simply be sentences that you construct. However, I would gather them randomly, without any thought as to whether or not they will lead easily to alternate meanings.

2. Select at least ten of the sentences and write two jokes for each of them that are based on an alternate meaning.

Jokes based on the primary meaning, the obvious interpretation, don't count.

HERE'S WHAT THIS WORKOUT WILL DO FOR YOU

This workout will show you that, with some effort, you can uncover hidden meanings in almost any grouping of words. At first, that may not seem possible because the obvious meaning leaps out at you. It overpowers you to the point where you believe it is the only meaning.

Then you begin to discover alternate interpretations. As you see them, you'll notice that it becomes easier and easier to spot them.

As you learn to look beyond the obvious and fight off the inclination to *accept* it, you'll become more skilled at creating humor.

HERE ARE SOME EXAMPLES

Below are three straightforward sentences:

1. "Do you cheat on your spouse?"

2. "Have you been a writer all your life?"

3. "Are you afraid of flying in an airplane?"

And here are a few replies that are based on the alternate meanings:

1A. "Certainly. Who else can I cheat on?"

1B. "If anybody's cheating on my spouse, it better be me."

★   ★   ★   ★   ★

2A. "No. In first and second grade I was a printer."

2B. "I hope not. I'm not dead yet."

★   ★   ★   ★   ★

3A. "No. If I'm going to fly, I prefer to use an airplane."

3B. "I find it's about the only useful thing one can do in an airplane."

★   ★   ★   ★   ★

A WORD BEFORE YOU START

Those examples should be clear. Each one shows how I misinterpreted the intended meaning of the questions. I found alternate meanings in them.

Not all of the jokes are of "performable" quality, but that's all right. This workout is simply practice in seeing and hearing sentences in a different way. That skill will lead to better comedy writing in all other areas.

Keep in mind that these are workouts. They're practice. They're like a musician reviewing the scales. The scales alone won't produce a symphony, but playing them sure helps.

Have fun with this workout.

= WORKOUT 6B =
"How Do I Get to Carnegie Hall?"

In this workout, you have more control, but that might only prove to be more of a challenge. Basically, this is the same as Workout 6A except that you compose the questions and write a joke answer to them that you think really works. That should produce better comedic results. In Workout 6A, you were primarily looking for alternative meanings; in this workout, you want more humor.

HERE'S WHAT YOU DO FOR THIS WORKOUT

Write 15 jokes in the question-and-comedy answer format, based on an alternative meaning of the question.

HERE'S WHAT THIS WORKOUT WILL DO FOR YOU

This workout will teach you how to create humor by beginning with a fun concept, finding the question that leads to the comedy, and phrasing the response.

HERE ARE SOME EXAMPLES

"If you were me, how would you play this golf shot?"
"Like I do everything else—magnificently."

★   ★   ★   ★   ★

"Why do you think that horse you bet on came in eighth?"
"Because there were only seven other horses in the race."

★   ★   ★   ★   ★

"Are you going to be cremated after you die?"
"I certainly wouldn't want to do it any sooner than that."

A WORD BEFORE YOU START

I'm admittedly prejudiced, but I think these examples have a bit more comedy than the ones from Workout 6A. That's because I wasn't locked into a random sentence. I designed the questions with an eye towards the humor content.

To give you an example, the last joke originally read as follows:

"In the next life, are you going to Heaven or Hell?"
"I suppose so. There don't seem to be any other options."

Then I thought that changing the question to "after you die" presented the opportunity for a funnier punchline, so I changed it to:

"Are you going to go to Heaven or Hell after you die?"
"I certainly don't want to go any sooner than that."

Then I felt that there's nothing wrong with going to Heaven for a two-week vacation and then coming back to this life, so I tried to find a question that led to a funnier picture. That's when I settled for the "cremation" set-up.

Obviously, in the previous workout we didn't have that luxury. So, go at this workout with some creativity, and stick with it. Have fun doing it, too.

= WORKOUT 6C =
"101 Tom Swifties"

When you read the requirements for completing this workout, you'll think I've gone masochistic. You'll swear it's too much work—almost impossible to complete—and not much fun in the process. You're wrong on all three counts.

I've given this exercise to many students and it always turns out to be the most popular. Many people complain at first that it's too much effort, but once they get into the swing of the workout, they can't stop—or rather, don't want to stop. They invariably produce more than the minimum requirements.

I've nicknamed this exercise "101 Tom Swifties" because you need to produce 101 of them, and because they're based on a grammatical form that was used in the writing of the "Tom Swift" books. That author used the "ly" form of the adverb often. ("Stop doing that," Tom shouted angri*ly*.)

However, in this workout, you're going to give an alternative meaning to the "ly" form of the adverb. You're going to convert it to another meaning. For instance:

"You put too much chili powder in this recipe," Tom said *hotly*.

The adverb, "hotly," normally used in this context would mean angrily. However, because of the sentence that precedes it, it takes on an alternative meaning. It means that the chili powder was burning his throat.

You can also play the Swiftie in another way. You can give alternative meanings to only parts of the word. For example:

"Your dog chased me down the driveway and tore my trousers," the mailman said deceitfully.

"Deceitfully" doesn't mean the mailman was lying; it means "de-seat-fully." The seat of his pants was chewed up by the dog.

Other than the fact that the key word must end in "ly," and that you need to apply some kind of alternative meaning to the key word, there are no rules. You may be—in fact, should be—as creative and innovative as you want.

The examples that follow will explain this more fully.

HERE'S WHAT YOU DO FOR THIS WORKOUT

Compose 101 "Tom Swifties." The "Tom Swifty" is defined as a quotation with a "ly" adverb describing the way the person speaks. The form is:

"I'll complete this workout, but it might take me seven days," the reader said weakly.

HERE'S WHAT THIS WORKOUT WILL DO FOR YOU

First, the requirement of 101 may seem pretty stiff, but it will teach discipline. That's an essential lesson for any writer, but especially a comedy writer.

There's another valuable lesson here—not giving up on an assignment too soon. It's the single most common fault of most beginning writers. They abandon the project too soon, before their best work is on paper. Stick with it. You'll see that as you get into this workout, you'll get caught up by it. As you have fun with it, you'll produce better material. (Trust me on that.)

That's a lesson for writers, too. Try to generate some enthusiasm for your project. It's practical and it improves your product.

HERE ARE SOME EXAMPLES

"Why don't we make this type darker than the rest?" the printer asked boldly.

Here we're using the word bold to mean brash and also heavy print. This joke is basically a pun. It's a wordplay on "bold." That's acceptable for this workout, but like most puns, it doesn't tell a story. It doesn't paint a graphic image in the listener's mind.

★   ★   ★   ★   ★

"Every time I see that cute little female insect, something tingly happens," the young lightning bug said glowingly.

This is a pun on the word, "glow," but it also tells a little story. It presents an image of an adolescent lightning bug who doesn't realize that his tail lights up when he's aroused.

★   ★   ★   ★   ★

"I do believe I'm sinking in quicksand," the explorer said defeatingly.

This is still a pun, but a more complex one, a more interesting one. And it does paint a funny image. "Defeat" means "de-feet, to remove one's feet." It paints a picture of a man glancing down to notice his feet have disappeared under the slime.

★   ★   ★   ★   ★

"I should have known better than to try to shove food down a lion's mouth," the animal trainer said offhandedly.

These are puns, too, but they present a graphic, if somewhat grotesque, image.

"I'm a performer at a topless club," the stripper said barely.

★   ★   ★   ★   ★

"I work at a bottomless club," another said cheekily.

★   ★   ★   ★   ★

"And I work for the Vice Squad," the policeman said arrestingly.

Here I had a little fun by tying several of the "Tom Swifties" together to tell a little story, with a surprise ending.

A WORD BEFORE YOU START

You get the idea. Be as wacky, as zany, as bizarre as you want, but do complete 101 of these. I guarantee you'll have fun with this one.

Chapter Seven

WORKING WITH OBSERVATION

I used to write a weekly column for a local paper. It was a humorous column, usually based on current events. I was late getting copy to the paper one weekend and had to come up with 10 or 12 witty comments before the end of the day. But I couldn't think of a topic to write about.

It was my morning for tennis, which I didn't want to miss, and it was also the day that John McEnroe was scheduled to play an important game at Wimbledon. I wanted to watch the telecast because McEnroe had been involved in a lot of controversy during the tournament. His antics covered the sports pages.

Even my family had planned to view the Wimbledon matches that afternoon. The publicity intrigued even those who didn't normally watch television sports.

I arrived at the tennis club without having decided on a topic, and obviously without having written any of the column. Everyone there was talking about McEnroe's behavior and planned to tune in to the match.

My family watched the games while I sat in my office struggling with my writing. What should I write about? Periodically someone would burst into my office with an updated report of the score and the shenanigans on court. Then my daughter innocently came up with the solution: "Dad, why don't you write abut Wimbledon?"

I felt like running naked through the streets shouting "Eureka!" Certainly that was the topic. Everybody was talking about it. Everyone would see it. It was the hot, current topic of the day. *And* it was easy to write about. I zipped off a column in minutes and went out to watch the finish of the match.

It had been the hot, current topic when I woke up in the morning. It had screamed at me from the first three pages of the morning paper's sports section. It had dominated conversation at the tennis club. It had captivated my family, normally non-tennis fans. But I hadn't seen it.

A major factor in humor is "recognition." A joke's effectiveness changes depending on that factor alone. To illustrate: a young lad on a high school football team spoke at a dinner honoring his coach. He told the audience that the coach and his wife recently returned from a trip to Europe, a second honeymoon. He said, "Coach isn't sure whether he had a good time or not. He has to wait to see the films."

That audience appreciated the gag, but the members of the football team enjoyed it more than anyone else. They recognized the significance of it more. They had often heard the coach say to them that he didn't know if they played well or not; he'd have to look at the game films first.

That joke wouldn't work nearly as well before an audience of detached business people. They wouldn't "feel" the relationship to it.

Television humorists have to discover topics that are universal, that everyone knows about and recognizes. Bob Hope and Johnny Carson do it by following the national headlines. They talk about what people are reading about and hearing about. Some other comics talk about what's on television—the shows or the commercials. Other young comics comment on universal topics like dating, school, getting a job, and the like.

All of these, though, require a keen sense of observation. Which headlines are hot? What's happening on TV? What experiences do I have in common with my audience? The more unique you can make your topics, and still retain that recognizability, the funnier your material will be.

Like me overlooking the John McEnroe topic, we all overlook valuable sources for humor. The raw material is there, we simply don't recognize it. We don't realize its usefulness.

George Carlin lives basically the same kind of life that you and I do. Yet he dissects it into humor. Robert Klein watches the same TV shows that we do, but he finds the irony in them. Carson reads the same headlines as the rest of the nation, but he uncovers the fun in them. Roseanne Barr is funny because she says about her marriage what many women want to say about theirs. She just thought to say it.

I watched Jay Leno do a funny routine about his Mom and Dad reacting to the new television set he bought them with a remote control unit. His Mom was afraid of it. She thought if she aimed it at the set and missed, she'd blow a hole in the wall. His Dad never used it because he didn't want to burn up the batteries. My Mom and Dad were the same way with new technology, but I never thought of doing a routine about it.

I saw Bill Cosby do a hilarious routine about his first pair of bifocals. When he left the doctor's office, everything was distorted. The elevator was 300 feet long and the people in it were only seven inches high. I laughed because I had the same experience. The difference is that Cosby noted it, wrote it, and performed it.

I've seen many young performers in comedy clubs and on television (and you probably have, too) do routines where I laughed and said, "Yeah, that's happened to me."

Funny, nonsensical, ironic things happen in all of our lives. They probably happen every day of our lives. Humorists find them, observe that they're funny and then mold them into comedy routines.

This group of workouts will help you to become more aware of the comedy that's happening around you. They will help you observe and then refine that comedy into presentable form. Then others can listen to you and say, "Doggone, that exact same thing happened to me."

= WORKOUT 7A =
"Truth Is Humor"

This workout is primarily research.

HERE'S WHAT YOU DO FOR THIS WORKOUT

Compile a list of 15 jokes that are basically observations. The gags should be little more than statements of fact, but those facts should be funny or ironic.

For example—"He who laughs last. . . ." One observation might be:

"He who laughs first probably told the joke."

It's funny, but it's also a recognizable truth. The gag line is simply stating the truth.

Use the jokes that you compiled in Chapter One, or research new lines, or simply list lines that you recall from your memory.

HERE'S WHAT THIS WORKOUT WILL DO FOR YOU

This workout shows you how other humorists use their observations to generate comedy. Notice that often the observation itself is the joke.

HERE ARE SOME EXAMPLES

When the audience groaned at one of Jack Benny's jokes at a rehearsal for his radio show, he quipped, "What are you complaining about? You all got in for free."

★　★　★　★　★

Gallagher was talking about the problems with today's mail delivery. Then he said, "But how about those Jehovah's Witnesses who always come to your door? Hey, I've got an idea! Why not let them deliver the mail? They're going to be in the neighborhood anyway."

★　★　★　★　★

David Brenner used this line in a routine he does about people asking stupid questions: "Excuse me, but are you reading that paper you're sitting on?"

★　★　★　★　★

George Carlin notes that people often use time to replace distance.

"How far do you have to drive to work?"

"Oh, just about 15 minutes."

He observes, though, that it's not interchangeable. It doesn't work when you use distance to replace time.

"What time do you have?"

"Oh, it's about three miles past noon."

A WORD BEFORE YOU START

None of the lines above needed any sort of rewrite from the comedian. They are funny as is. Very little "writing" had to be done. Once the observation was made, the jokes practically wrote themselves.

Have fun with this workout.

= WORKOUT 7B =

"What You See Is What You Laugh At"

In this workout you will practise looking for the ironies, the contradictions, the fun in everyday life. You will call upon your powers of observation.

HERE'S WHAT YOU DO FOR THIS WORKOUT

Compile a list of 15 observations that have the potential for humor from any number of different areas of everyday life. These observations don't have to be jokes; they simply should be truths that lend themselves to humor.

You may list any facet of everyday life that will be easily recognized by ordinary people. Here is a list that may help to get you started, but you may draw from any area.

parents	marriage	driving
dating	raising children	your workplace

HERE'S WHAT THIS WORKOUT WILL DO FOR YOU

Completing this workout should sharpen your powers of observation.

This workout, too, should illustrate that there is humor in almost any situation. It doesn't always pop out at you, but it's there if you train yourself to look hard enough.

HERE ARE SOME EXAMPLES

Here are some of the ironies that I've noted about my Mom:

Mom would give me spending money when I went on a school picnic, and then get angry when I spent it.

★　★　★　★　★

When I was getting ready to go on an excursion, Mom would tell me to have fun and then forbid me to do any of the things that were fun.

★　★　★　★　★

Mom would take anything that was valuable and say, "I'm going to put this in a safe place." Then she'd forget where she put it.

★　★　★　★　★

When I was a kid, Mom would always yell, "Be quiet or you'll wake your Father," loud enough to wake my father.

★　★　★　★　★

When Mom got older she would never wear any of the new clothes we would buy her. She wanted them always to be new.

A WORD BEFORE YOU START

These were idiosyncrasies of my mother, but I'm sure you recognize a few of them. You can probably rattle off a dozen more of them about your mom, too. All of these are fodder for your humor.

Learn to observe the humor around you and incorporate it into your writing.

Have fun doing this research.

= WORKOUT 7C =
"Observation Field Trip"

This workout is more pointed. It's a kind of field trip in observation. In it you purposely put yourself in a situation where you can study people and that leads to observations about them.

HERE'S WHAT YOU DO FOR THIS WORKOUT

1. Decide on an area that you will research. You can make this a part of your everyday life. For example, if you are a student, you might observe what people do in the classroom as the teacher lectures. If you take an exercise class, you might observe the others as they work out. Or you might place yourself in an arena that is foreign to your everyday schedule. You might go to the airport, for instance, and report on how people dress to travel, or what sort of luggage they haul around.

Here are examples of a few areas that you might study. These are only starter suggestions. Select your own.

How people behave on public transportation.

Idiosyncrasies of people walking their dogs.

The behavior of people in the lobby of a movie theatre. (Do they buy food? What food? And so on.)

In any case, pick a specific topic for your research.

2. Do the study and gather at least ten observations.

HERE'S WHAT THIS WORKOUT WILL DO FOR YOU

This workout will be invaluable training in gathering material for your comedy writing. It will teach you that you can select almost any area to write about, because—if you study it deeply enough—you'll uncover humor, or at least the potential for humor in it.

HERE ARE SOME EXAMPLES

I selected people travelling by air for my study. Here are a few of my observations:

1. Some people struggled onto the plane carrying four, five, or six items that hardly fit on the plane, let alone in the overhead compartment.

2. A businessman was carrying a suitbag that was so overloaded that it threatened to burst. The bag was designed to carry a suit and a few overnight items, but this gentleman has it loaded with enough for a month's stay.

3. At least one person, despite the illuminated seat belt sign and repeated warnings from the flight attendants, jumped up as soon as the wheels bumped the ground, gathered his belongings and then had to stand and wait until the doors opened for deplaning.

4. Some people moved my stuff around in the overhead bin so that their stuff fit in more conveniently.

5. Some folks listened to the comedy channel on the headset and laughed uproariously, completely unaware that most of the rest of the folks on the plane were laughing at them laughing at the comedy albums.

A WORD BEFORE YOU START

You may notice that most of these people are recognizable to anyone who travels by air. Most of them are on every plane.

You'll probably agree, too, that a comedy routine or a humorous article could be written about any one or all of them collectively.

You will probably have the same realizations about the observation you make on your study, too.

This is an interesting workout. Have fun with it.

= WORKOUT 7D =
"You Know It's Time To ... When ..."

In this workout, you will use your powers of observation, coupled with your creativity and sense of humor, to write jokes.

The form will be: "You know it's time to (blank) when ..." You'll fill in the punchline.

For example:

"You know it's time to leave the amusement park when ..."

"You know it's time to buy a new car when ..."

"You know it's time to go on a diet when ..."

You may change the form slightly if you wish. It can be something like:

"You know you're about to be fired when ..."

"You know someone's car is brand new when ..."

HERE'S WHAT YOU DO FOR THIS WORKOUT

1. Decide on the topic that you will write your observational jokes about, and then construct the opening line of your joke. (The opening line that will apply to all your jokes is the "You know ..." line.)

2. Create 10 to 15 punchlines that go with your opening line. The punchlines you write can go a little bit beyond pure observation. However, they should be based on truth and be recognizable to most readers or listeners.

HERE'S WHAT THIS WORKOUT WILL DO FOR YOU

This workout will give you practical experience in using your observational skills to write jokes. It will be valuable practice in analyzing a specific situation in order to extract the humor from it.

HERE ARE SOME EXAMPLES

You know your child has misbehaved in school once too often when. . . .

. . . you get a note from the principal that says, "Please meet me at the school tomorrow at 10 o'clock. A Sheriff's car will be by at 9:45 to pick you up."

★ ★ ★ ★ ★

. . . you receive word that your child will miss dinner this evening. He is being kept after school. . . . until the year 1997.

★ ★ ★ ★ ★

. . . you receive notice that your child has not only been expelled, but also deported.

A WORD BEFORE YOU START

All of those examples are exaggerations, but exaggerations based on truthful observations. The premise is finding out that your child has gone overboard in his mischievous behavior at school. The joke examples are based on ordinary things that do happen when children misbehave. The parents are invited to a meeting, the children are kept after school and sometimes they're expelled.

There are other things that happen when children are naughty in school. They have to write out a resolution, do extra homework, sit in a corner, wear a dunce cap. Each of these might lead to a joke.

This is a practical example of the use of observation in writing a comedy routine.

This workout should be challenging, so have some fun with it.

Chapter Eight

WORKING WITH ANALYZATION

Suppose you were to emcee a dinner honoring your boss's 25 years with the company. He is the manager of your accounting department and you want to "roast" him in a friendly manner. You want a line that gently kids him about his accounting skills. You might say:

> "Our guest of honor is to accounting what Oprah Winfrey is to pole vaulting."

It's a wacky, funny line that probably would get big laughs from this audience. "But," you say, "I'm afraid to use that line because Oprah has gone on a diet and the women in the audience might consider it sexist . . ." Okay, then we'll change it to:

> "Our guest of honor is to accounting what Dom DeLuise is to pole vaulting."

It doesn't hurt the joke that much, and it avoids the sexist criticism. "But," you say, "I don't want to pick on overweight people. There may be some in the audience who could be offended." Okay, then we'll change it to:

> "Our guest of honor is to accounting what Willie Shoemaker is to professional basketball."

Same idea, but it eliminates the concerns you have. "But," you say, "it doesn't sound as funny as pole vaulting." Okay, then let's try a different approach.

I'll give you a joke that I used years ago at a Friar's roast. It went like this:

> "Our guest of honor is to accounting what Bobby Fischer is to chess—a real pain in the ass."

"But," you say, "Who the hell is Bobby Fischer?" Well, he was an American chess champion who defeated the Russian champion for the World Championship of Chess back around 1971–72. Fischer was a real renegade who broke every known rule of chess etiquette so the matches were on the front pages of the daily newspapers for several weeks. Well, it was a funny line at the time. . . .

"But," you say, "This dinner is now. No one will know what I'm talking about." Okay, so let's update the line:

> "Our guest of honor is to accounting what John McEnroe is to tennis—a real pain in the ass."

There. We've salvaged the line by substituting a more current name. "But," you say, "it's not that much more current. McEnroe hasn't played top tennis for awhile. Besides not everyone in the audience is familiar with tennis." Okay, then I'm stymied. I have no more references.

Write your own opening line.

It should kid your guest of honor goodnaturedly, and if the reference is right, it will get big laughs. It will also set the tone for the evening—friendly, barbless banter.

The key words there are "if the reference is right." We just took this joke through five punchlines, none of which pleased you. How then can you write a new one?

Actually, it would be easy if you had a list of 50 to 75 references of this type. If such a list existed, you could just glance at it, select the one that fit this joke perfectly, and write it in.

"But," you say (you're starting to get on my nerves with that "but"), "where can I get such a list?"

There's the rub. You have to create it. You have to think about it, let it meander through your mind, jot down any ideas you have, and generate your own list. Not all of the references will be good; not all of them will work as the punchline to this joke. But one of them should, and that's all you need.

That's what is meant by "analyzation."

We've already seen that a joke is usually composed of two interrelated parts called the "setup" and the "punchline." The first part is a slow-moving process. It's the part we talked about and practised in the workouts in Chapter Seven. It's usually a slow, methodical effort to find what we will make the setup for our joke.

The second part, though, is a lightning fast, computer-like process of scanning and evaluating relationships that go with that setup. We roll thoughts through our brains almost quicker than we can think of them. And we reject many of them just as quickly. Then our mind settles on one that might make a joke. The mind presents it to us and says, "Here's your joke; refine the wording."

It seems reasonable that the more ideas we have to scan, the better our chances of finding a joke, and the better the joke will be.

In our example, we suggested five associations. None of them were satisfactory. If we had ten to select from, we might have found a usable joke. If we had 100 to study, we might have found a better joke. And if we had 10,000 choices available, we'd probably have located the ideal joke.

By analyzing our topic, we're presenting our mind with as many options as we can. Not all of them will be used, but that's all right. Having the list will still provide us with the punchlines we need quickly and with relative ease.

Some of the punchlines we think of won't come from the list. Again, that's all right because the list is generating another list subconsciously. As you begin writing, it stimulates your mind to think of even more associations.

Do all gag-writers go through this association procedure? Yes. Do all professional writers make a list before beginning to write their gagas? No. That's because they become so proficient at writing punchlines that they can run through a list of associations without jotting them down.

Should you make a list? Yes. It's good practice to get your mind thinking of associations, and they are the heart of joke writing. Secondly, it will speed up the plateau-jumping of a comedy writer. You'll be able to move much more quickly to that time when you won't have to jot down all of your thoughts as preparation.

Again, remember that these are workouts to develop and strengthen your writing skills. Be faithful to them now and they'll pay dividends later. The musicians whose fingers fly over the keyboard attained that skill by plodding through the exercises in their earlier training.

= WORKOUT 8A =
"Random Associations"

This workout gives you practice in letting your mind ramble through any topic and come up with random associations that may or may not be used later as setups or punchlines for jokes.

The items that you generate in this workout don't have to be funny. In fact, they don't even have to be too closely related to your topic. It's almost a free association exercise. If your topic is "hunting" and your mind says you should jot down "whales," don't fret, don't censor, don't question; jot it down. Who knows? It just might lead to a "Moby Dick" or "Captain Ahab" line that *does* tie in with your "hunting" premise.

Trust me on this first workout. When we do the other workouts in this chapter, it will all tie together.

HERE'S WHAT YOU DO FOR THIS WORKOUT

1. Select a topic or premise that you will write about. It's your choice, but make it definite. Make it broad, but not so broad that it's unwieldy.

2. With a pencil and paper, or a typewriter or word processor, write down in no particular order (and without editorializing, censoring, or reprimanding yourself), any words, phrases, people, places, or things—anything at all—that you feel relate in any way to your premise.

Continue until you have at least 50 such items.

HERE'S WHAT THIS WORKOUT WILL DO FOR YOU

Making the list prepares your mind to write on your topic. You will be forcing yourself to think about your topic, almost to the exclusion of everything else. That's a big plus for a writer. It's a discipline we all need.

As you make random associations, your subconscious mind will also be selecting different angles to look at your topic from. You'll find that useful when you move on to writing.

When you finally get around to creating jokes, you will have a wealth of ammunition that you can draw on for those oh-so-important associations that form the heart of comedy writing.

HERE ARE SOME EXAMPLES

I've selected the topic "Buying a car." Here are the random thoughts I jotted down:

tax and license	stick shift
dealer prep	power steering/windows/locks
test drive	windshield wipers
trade-in	whitewall tires
kicking the tires	tinted windows
sticker price	warranty

factory air (conditioning)
options
factory rebate
making a deal
financing
make and model
car salesman
showroom floor
four on the floor
"car of the year"
Car and Driver Magazine
shopping around
"Make me an offer"
"Would I lie to you?"
"Used by a little old lady
    who drove it back and
    forth to church"
"I can't do any better"
"drive it off the lot"
racing stripe

mileage
trunk space
"comes equipped with"
lemon
"goes from zero to fifty"
handles beautifully
hugs the road
stops on a dime
turning radius
engine hum
"Take it to your mechanic"
"Sign here"
insurance
2- or 4-door
6- or 8-cylinder
cruise control
leather interior
roomy interior
new car smell
mag wheels

A WORD BEFORE YOU START

That list is typical. It includes many items that almost anyone would include in such a collection. It might also have a few that no one else would have included—things that only I would think about in buying a car. Then, too, it might have a few that seem disconnected to car buying. That's okay. That's the writer's privilege.

Is this a good list, a mediocre list, or a bad list? Who knows? There's no judgment required for this list. It is designed to get the writer thinking about the topic and to furnish ammunition for the actual writing, which comes later.

So attack this workout with gusto, and have fun with it.

= WORKOUT 8B =
"Focused List of Associations"

This workout is similar to Workout 8A, except more focused. In the previous workout, you allowed your creativity to wander through the topic without direction or interference. It was free association.

In this workout, you'll focus on certain facets of your premise and try to extract even more associations.

The purpose is the same—to gather more information that might be useful when you begin the writing process.

HERE'S WHAT YOU DO FOR THIS WORKOUT

1. Use the same premise you selected for Workout 8A.

2. Design a form that includes spaces for the following:

Similar to your premise:	*Opposite to your premise:*
people	people
places	places
things	things
events	events
words, phrases, clichés	words, phrases, clichés

You may write these associations in any form you choose. You can use different areas of a scratch pad, generate a typed form on your word processor, or draw up a ruled form and have it reproduced.

This is a format that I use.

	SIMILAR	OPPOSITE
WORDS, PHRASES, CLICHÉS		
EVENTS		
THINGS		
PLACES		
PEOPLE		

3. Fill each blank with at least 3 selections having to do with your premise.

HERE'S WHAT THIS WORKOUT WILL DO FOR YOU

You'll discover that as you narrow your focus, you increase your productivity. You keep your mind concentrating on a particular area. That enables you to uncover even more associations.

HERE ARE SOME EXAMPLES

I've kept my previous topic, "Buying a car." The form below shows the new associations I've come up with in this workout.

	SIMILAR	OPPOSITE
WORDS, PHRASES, CLICHES	"DAD, CAN I BORROW THE CAR" / "Is that the ONLY COLOR THEY COME IN?" / "TAKE HER OUT FOR A SPIN."	"The warranty doesn't cover that." / "They'll do that on you." / "We don't know what is wrong with it."
EVENTS	INDY 500 / FIRST SCRATCH / BRINGING NEW CAR HOME TO THE FAMILY	ACCIDENT / REPOSSESSION / HITCH-HIKE
THINGS	WINDSHIELD WIPERS / HOOD ORNAMENT / CAR KEYS	HITCHING POST / STABLE / HORSE CART
PLACES	DETROIT / TEST TRACK / ASSEMBLY LINE	MATTEL TOY FACTORY / LEMON GROVE / NASA LAUNCH PAD
PEOPLE	FORD, HENRY / LINCOLN / JOHN DE LOREAN	WOODY ALLEN (DOESN'T DRIVE) / RALPH NADER / BUS DRIVER

A WORD BEFORE YOU START

Again, no evaluation is possible for this completed form. The items that I included may or may not help me find setups and punchlines for the gags I will eventually have to write. They will be there, though, as a support and a creative stimulant when I get into the process of writing the humor. So persevere through this exercise, and have fun with it.

ASSOCIATIONS FORM

	SIMILAR	OPPOSITE
WORDS, PHRASES, CLICHES		
EVENTS		
THINGS		
PLACES		
PEOPLE		

You can photocopy this form, or make up your own.

= WORKOUT 8C =
"A Specific Associations List"

This workout is a combination of Workouts 8A and 8B, except that in those you selected your own topic, and in this workout you'll work on a pre-assigned topic. The process you go through, however, will be exactly the same.

Your pre-assigned topic will be "exercising."

HERE'S WHAT YOU DO FOR THIS WORKOUT

1. Make a free association list of items related to the topic of "exercising." Work until your list is reasonably extensive. I would not stop at less than 50 items.

2. Complete an Associations form (see page 78) with people, places, things, events and phrases that are both similar and opposite to the main premise, "exercising."

Again, make this list reasonably complete. I would recommend having at least three items in each area.

3. Save these lists because you use them again in the next workout.

A WORD BEFORE YOU START

Since these workouts are the same as 8A and 8B, you won't need any explanation, examples, or summations. Let's save that until you complete Workout 8D, which is a continuation of this one.

Have fun completing this, and then move ahead.

= WORKOUT 8D =
"Writing from Your Associations List"

This workout will finally get you to that writing process we've mentioned so many times throughout this chapter. Here you'll get to reap the benefits of the preparatory work you've been doing. You're going to write punchlines to given setups. They should lie somewhere in the lists you've been compiling.

HERE'S WHAT YOU DO FOR THIS WORKOUT

Write two punchlines each to the setup lines that follow. You don't have to draw from the items that you've listed, but do refer to them for inspiration.

You may change the setup line, if necessary, to accommodate the grammar, the rhythm, or the comedy of your punchline.

For example, the following line . . .

"I'm in really bad shape. Some people get up and touch their toes in the morning. I count mine."

. . . may be changed to accommodate a different punchline. For example . . .

"I'm in really bad shape. Some people touch their toes without bending their knees. I can't touch my knees without bending my toes."

Here are some setups for you to add punchlines to:

1. I hate to exercise. The only jogging I do is . . .

2. When I think of breaking out in a sweat, I . . .

3. My idea of a brisk workout is to . . .

4. Some people jump out of bed in the morning and touch their toes ten times. I jump out of bed in the morning and . . .

5. Some folks exercise and get big muscles. I exercise and get . . .

6. I'm in very bad shape. I went to the gym, and . . .

7. I asked the instructor what I should do to improve my figure (physique). He (she) recommended . . .

8. I've been doing sit-ups faithfully now for five weeks. The only change I've noticed is . . .

9. My instructor keeps saying, "No pain, no gain." I finally told him (her), ". . ."

10. The only exercise I really enjoy is the rowing machine (or substitute another exercise device). With that, at least I . . .

HERE'S WHAT THIS WORKOUT WILL DO FOR YOU

First of all, you're writing punchlines. Writing is always good practice for future writing.

Second, you're experiencing firsthand the value of a comprehensive list. Each of these setup lines is a challenge—and not an easy challenge. The ideas that are in your list, and the ideas that are suggested by the items in your list, should be an invaluable help in finding the correct punchline for each of these straight-lines.

HERE ARE SOME EXAMPLES

I don't want to offer any punchlines for the setups that I've given. That would only make your writing more difficult. So I've composed an eleventh straight-line and will furnish a few examples of punchlines that might be attached to it.

The setup is:

A friend of mine went to a health club and lost 25 pounds in no time. What happened was . . .

Here are some possible punchlines:

a) . . . one of those machines tore her leg off.

b) . . . somebody stole his gym bag.

c) . . . she got so exhausted from exercising, she fell asleep in the sauna.

d) . . . they made him check his lunch bag at the door.

e) . . . she paid cash.

A WORD BEFORE YOU START

You can probably recognize that any list I compiled would probably contain "exercise machines," "gym bag," "sauna or steam room." The straight-line and a study of the lists prompted the first three punchlines.

I also had the words "diet" and "expensive" on my lists, and they generated the last two lines. Although they are variations, they still were derived from the list.

However, the real awakening is in your own writing. You experience how the ammunition you gathered by compiling those extensive lists of associations helped you in writing your punchlines.

They should help the quality, quantity, and speed of your creativity. Put this theory to the test by completing this workout, and have fun with it.

= BONUS WORKOUT 8E =
"Finish the Joke"

We began this chapter with a joke setup that we never really resolved. The joke began:

"Our guest of honor is to accounting what . . ."

Then we tried to find some references that were funny because they were so incongruous.

Now that you see the benefit of having a list at your fingertips, and since that is a re-usable joke form, you might compile a list of 15 such references.

I'll get you started with a few, then the rest of this workout is up to you.

1. Dracula is to a balanced diet.

★   ★   ★   ★   ★

2. Quasimodo is to good posture.

★   ★   ★   ★   ★

3. Mr. Rogers is to the world of wrestling.

★   ★   ★   ★   ★

4. Colonel Kadaffi is to the Dale Carnegie course.

★   ★   ★   ★   ★

5. The Frankenstein monster is to tap dancing.

Keep going and have fun in the process.

Chapter Nine

WORKING WITH TOPICS AND SUBTOPICS

Television is an inflexible medium for the writer because the deadlines are so unyielding. A weekly show goes on the same day and the same time each week. The writing must be done in time to get the show on the air.

There's the story of a producer who poked his head into the writers' room to deliver a brief pep talk. "Let's make that sketch for this week's show really fantastic." One writer answered, "Make up your mind. Do you want it good or do you want it by Friday?"

Any writing you do should be good. Quality is supreme, but other factors are important, too. A brilliantly funny sketch that's delivered on Monday morning for last Friday night's show is obviously useless. Speed is not always important, but it sometimes is.

Quantity, too, is often essential. Why? Because it enhances quality. Let me explain. Suppose you have to deliver five lines at some important banquet. Naturally, you want the best five lines you can get. If you are a wealthy person, you can hire 20 good comedy writers to each write 100 lines for you. You now have 2,000 lines from which to select the five best. The chances are you're going to have five good lines. Because of the quantity, the quality of the five lines can improve.

The workouts in this chapter will show you a "shortcut" that will help you increase your writing speed and the quantity of writing you do. Consequently, it will improve the quality of your writing.

The "shortcut" consists of breaking your premise into bite-sized chunks. Instead of working on an overall topic, you divide that topic into several subtopics.

If you walk into a roomful of comedy writers and toss out a workable premise, they'll immediately ad-lib a half dozen punchlines. Most of us who write comedy can quickly toss that many lines off the top of our heads.

Try it yourself right now. Come up with a few lines on how bad airline food is. Don't edit or rewrite or criticize your lines too much; just try to toss out five or six quips about airline food. You should find it fairly easy.

However, if you walked into a roomful of comedy writers and said, "Give me 30 lines on any premise," they'd probably throw you out. They don't have that kind of time to waste.

You see, writing 30 or 35 lines on any one topic is overwhelming. It feels like there aren't that many jokes available on one topic. It's staggering. It defeats you before you even begin.

Because it feels impossible, you begin the project with a negative attitude. You think you can't do it, which makes it that much harder.

If instead of thinking about writing 30 jokes on one topic, you turn it into writing five or six jokes about five or six different topics—it suddenly becomes manageable.

If you do five lines about airline food, and five more about overhead luggage racks, followed by five jokes about late flights, then five more jokes about lost luggage, add in five gags about unpleasant flight attendants, and finish it off with five punchlines about the safety of flying; you now have a 30-joke routine about "Air Travel."

You may say that you've watched all the young comics on TV and none of them does that many jokes about one particular topic. True. But the jokes they do are usually pretty good. Quantity enhances quality.

By writing 30 or 35 lines, you now have the luxury of dropping the weaker lines. You can now get rid of two-thirds of your work and still have 10 usable lines.

The speed of the writing enhances the quality, too. If you find the 10 remaining lines aren't quite strong enough, you can add more subtopics and repeat the procedure. That should give you several more quality lines to add to your routine.

With this technique, you're making your comedy writing easier, quicker, and you're playing the percentages to make it better. The next time you watch Johnny Carson's monologue on television, count the jokes. He may do 25 of them.

Carson may have a staff of 8 to 12 writers working on each day's monologue. Do you think they only submitted 25 jokes? Of course not. They turned in at least ten times that amount. Carson filtered out the best. If he didn't get enough good lines, you can be sure he told the writers to try again—to submit more lines.

That's the technique the good comedians use to make sure they step on stage with only the best. You as a writer can use the same technique. Remember, it doesn't matter how many gags you throw away. What's important is how many you sell.

Here's how this subtopic "shortcut" works:

You decide on a main topic and then analyze it, breaking it into five or six subtopics. The subtopics would be a part of the main topic. For example, earlier we talked about "airline travel" as our main topic. The subtopics were:

    a) how bad airline food is

    b) overhead luggage compartments

    c) late flights

    d) unpleasant flight attendants

    e) the safety of flying

These are arbitrary facets that I selected as examples. There are no rules in choosing subtopics. There could just as well have been:

    a) terminology people use in flying

    b) the way people dress to fly

    c) ways to keep busy on an airplane

    d) people you've met while flying

    e) travelling to and from the airport

Either one of these groupings or a combination of both can produce workable material. The subtopics are a way of focusing your creative attention on one area and also overcoming fear at the immensity of your task.

You needn't stick with one subtopic until it's completed. Jump around as much as you like, but it is a nice scorecard to return to. When you find yourself pressed, glance at your subtopics and focus on just one of them.

Also, don't limit your creative juices once they start flowing. If you find that you can write 20, 30, or even 40 jokes on just one subtopic, go with it. You can always use the others as the beginning of another routine. You might surprise yourself and get two workable monologues for the price of one.

Give these workouts your best effort. I think you'll find that they'll help your creativity and your productivity.

= WORKOUT 9A =
"Fast and Funny"

This first workout is a speed exercise.

HERE'S WHAT YOU DO FOR THIS WORKOUT

1. Select a topic, making it as specific as you can. For instance, instead of "going to the movies," write about "how much they charge for refreshments in the lobby." Instead of "heavy traffic," you might do jokes about "how close the cars behind you get."

Here are a few topics to help you get started:

   a) how hard the biscuits you bake are

   b) how many names your spouse called you during an argument

   c) how bad the airline food is

   d) how dirty your hands get after reading the morning paper

   e) what some cheap friend will do to avoid picking up a lunch check

2. Write at least five jokes on your selected premise within 15 minutes. If you don't get them done in that amount of time, select another topic. Keep going until you complete five jokes within 15 minutes. If you are successful, either go through and try it a few more times, or move on to the next workout.

Don't spend a lot of time polishing your jokes or being too critical. This is a workout to increase speed. In fact, you don't even have to write out the entire joke. A key word jotted on a piece of paper is all you need for this particular workout. As long as the joke is in your head, you can write it out and perhaps improve it later.

Don't give up on this one too early. It may take a few tries to accomplish this "speed writing," but it's excellent practice and well worth the effort.

HERE'S WHAT THIS WORKOUT WILL DO FOR YOU

You'll prove to yourself that you can write quickly. Also, this is excellent training for letting creativity flow freely and for discovering that a positive approach to your task influences the results.

HERE ARE SOME EXAMPLES

It's difficult to give examples for an ad-lib, top-of-the-head workout such as this. But I'll list five gags that I came up with within 15 minutes just to show you the type of lines that you might generate.

My topic was "how badly I played tennis today." Here goes:

"I should have just stopped playing. My partner asked me to about eight or nine times."

     ★   ★   ★   ★   ★

"My tennis was so bad today if it was alive, it would have been put to sleep."

     ★   ★   ★   ★   ★

I asked the pro what I was doing wrong. He said, "Damn near everything."

★   ★   ★   ★   ★

"I asked the pro if he could help my game." He said, "I'm sorry. Our club doesn't have an intensive care unit."

★   ★   ★   ★   ★

When we finished playing I said, "Now I have to go home and write jokes." My partner said, "It's going to be tough for you to be funnier than this."

(Just for the record, and as a sort of encouragement, these lines took about six minutes.)

A WORD BEFORE YOU START

Remember this is a speed workout. The lines you jot down may not be complete, but they are good raw material. With more time, you may be able to refine them or combine them into good, solid comedy one-liners. The polishing and rewriting can come later. Right now you just want to generate quick comedy ideas.

It's important to note in this workout that the freer your mind is, the faster the lines will pop into your head. If you're afraid that you can't complete the exercise, you become inhibited. That blocks the creative process and chances are you won't complete it. Once you put aside that fear, though, and approach the workout with a positive attitude, the jokes happen.

The same is true of most writing tasks. The more you fear them, the harder they are to complete. The more you back off from a project, the more difficult it becomes to do the job well.

Learn from this workout to attack each project with gusto, free from fear. Then stand back and enjoy it.

= WORKOUT 9B =
"Topics to Subtopics"

In this workout, you'll get some practice in dissecting a topic into several subtopics. There are no hard and fast rules about how to do it. Any subtopic will serve the purpose so long as it helps you to focus your creative energy and to divide the main topic into manageable pieces.

HERE'S WHAT YOU DO FOR THIS WORKOUT

Divide each of the following topics into six subtopics that relate to it.

a) Eating out   c) Gardening   e) The governor of your state

b) Your parents   d) Working for a mean boss

Note: Save the lists you make. You may want to use them for later workouts.

HERE'S WHAT THIS WORKOUT WILL DO FOR YOU

This workout is practice in all the things we've been talking about in this chapter. It also forces you to do some of the preparatory work that helps your writing.

HERE ARE SOME EXAMPLES

My topic is bringing home a new puppy. Here are the subtopics:

a) how much it wets

b) how much it eats

c) how much it whined the first night

d) how quickly you fall in love with it

e) how quickly it gets its own way

f) how it's more trouble than children

A WORD BEFORE YOU START

The example is very subjective. People dissect a premise based on personal experience and feelings. Some might never get attached to such a troublesome little creature, and would change item (d) to "how I'm trying to find ways to get rid of it without upsetting the family."

Both these subtopics are valid. They are different approaches to the same problem. They help you to examine your views on the main premise, list them, and then use that list to focus your writing.

So, jot down whatever pops into your mind, and have fun with this workout.

= WORKOUT 9C =
"More Topics to Subtopics"

This workout is exactly the same as 9B except that you select your own main topics to subdivide.

= WORKOUT 9D =
"Writing Fast and Funny from Subtopics"

This workout will put the previous three exercises to the acid test. Here you'll try to write jokes for each of your subtopics, put them together, and form a 30–35 joke routine on one main premise.

HERE'S WHAT YOU DO FOR THIS WORKOUT

1. Select any list of subtopics that you generated in either Workout 9B or Workout 9C.

2. Write at least five jokes for each subtopic.

HERE'S WHAT THIS WORKOUT WILL DO FOR YOU

This will prove that you can write 30 jokes on a given premise—and that you can do it quickly. Of course, you don't have to follow the time restriction we set up in Workout 9A. You can take longer than 15 minutes to write your jokes.

This one exercise, repeated a few times, will do wonders in increasing your output and also upgrading the quality of your comedy writing.

HERE ARE SOME EXAMPLES

The examples from the previous three workouts should give you a good idea of the kind of writing you need to do here.

A WORD BEFORE YOU START

In this workout you've generated enough material for a monologue. Following the steps in this chapter is not essential to writing a monologue, but it is very helpful. I recommend going through this procedure any time you have to write one-liners that are to be part of a routine.

They focus your writing, make it easier and quicker to write well, and benefit the overall quality of your work. I suggest you make them a part of your writing always.

Though you've generated enough material, you don't have a finished monologue yet. In later chapters we'll discuss rewrites and transitions that will help blend this material into a completed comedy routine.

Save the material you create in this workout.

Have fun with it.

Chapter Ten

WORKING WITH JOKE WRITING

The question producers ask writers in Hollywood is "Can you put it on paper?" The buyers don't really care if you're wacky at parties, if you're quick with a comeback, if you can insult strangers without inhibition. None of that matters. That's your personality, your lifestyle, your hang-up, or whatever. What makes you a writer is the words you put on the paper.

There's a difference between thinking funny, being funny, and *writing* funny—a big difference. Writing is communicating. It's converting an idea you have into words that convey that idea to readers or listeners. The idea is not enough.

For instance, let's say we have an idea that there is both good and evil in all people. We give that idea to several people. We'll get some terrible essays, short stories, and novels based on that premise. We'll also get some good ones. But not everyone will convert it into a masterpiece the way Robert Louis Stevenson did with *Dr. Jekyll and Mr. Hyde*.

Comedy writers, too, have to "put it on paper." They have to convert the preparatory work—the planning, the plotting, the analyzing, the comparing—to writing. Sooner or later, comedy writers have to get to the comedy.

The workouts in this chapter will help get your mind thinking "joke."

One criticism we hear about teaching comedy writing is "You can't teach someone to be funny." That's true. But you can teach someone tricks of the trade that will help them to use the "funny" that they already have.

You certainly can't teach anyone to be stronger, either. A person has only so much strength. Yet, if you take a person with power, and send him or her to a good weightlifting coach, that person will be able to lift more than without the coach.

Did the coach make the person stronger? No. But he or she taught technique— taught that person how to use the strength that was already there more effectively.

That's what these workouts will do for the comedy writer.

Just as weightlifters can improve performance with proper training techniques, balance, breathing, and concentration; comedy writers can improve their writing by learning technique.

These workouts won't make you funnier, but they will make your writing funnier. They will stimulate your mind to migrate toward the funny. They'll focus your creative energy on "funny," just the way a power lifter concentrates on "the lift."

These workouts will teach you to think in ways that will help you to extract the humor from any premise you select. They won't do any of the work for you, but they'll help you to do the work on your own.

We'll discuss three basic techniques that should help you think funny. The first is making statements about your topic and then captioning these statements. We worked with this technique in Chapter Three, except there we captioned visuals. We worked with photos, drawings, and other graphic images.

We saw in Chapter Three that we could generate humor if we had a straight-line to work with. The straight-line in that chapter was visual. Here we're manufacturing our own straight-lines with factual statements.

The statements we list don't have to be funny. They're usually more effective if they're not. That way they provide more of a contrast with the punchline—more of a surprise.

The statements should be facts, ideas about the basic premise that we can use as raw material for our comic punchlines.

The second technique is to ask questions about the main premise. By asking questions we generate even more ammunition for our minds to work with. How does this idea affect other people? How does it affect us? What effect will it have on the future? What effect did it have in the past? Will it last? What would it be if we changed it? There are an infinite number of questions we can ask about practically any topic, and the answers to those questions stimulate our thinking. They force us to fantasize.

When questions like these are asked in a court of law, the attorney invariably shouts, "Objection. That calls for conjecture." In a court of law they don't want that; as creative writers we do. We want to conjure up all sorts of fantasies, daydreams, unbelievable situations. Asking questions helps us to do that. It helps us be creative and funny.

The third technique is to use a joke formula and then fill in the blanks. This sounds terribly uncreative but it isn't. All comedians and in fact all writers use formulas. The formula itself doesn't make something trite or cliché; it's how you fill in the blanks.

"It was so cold out my teeth were chattering" is a cliché, but it's also a formula. When Carson's writers take that same formula and say, "It was so cold out that flashers were just describing themselves," it becomes a joke. Hope's writers used the same formula to write, "It was so cold out that in New York the Statue of Liberty was holding the torch *under* her gown."

Some people condemn formula writing. They say, "There are only seven basic jokes," or, "There's no such thing as a new joke." That's silly. Formulas don't restrict creativity; they offer it another avenue. There are only 11 different notes on a musical scale, but they can be used in combinations that create beautiful, enchanting melodies—all different.

In the following workouts we'll learn to use statements, questions, and formulas to help you think funny.

= WORKOUT 10A =
"Statements to Jokes"

In this workout, you study a topic and extract factual statements that may provide fodder for your comedy material.

HERE'S WHAT YOU DO FOR THIS WORKOUT

1. Select a premise from the daily paper. You may take it from the front page, the sports page, the financial page, or anywhere in between. The premise you select should be written about in the paper at some length. In other words, don't pick a single paragraph item, but one that takes up at least several inches of newsprint.

2. Read through the article and select at least ten different statements that you might use for your comedy writing. List these on a separate sheet of paper.

3. Using the factual statements you listed, write punchlines for at least three of them. Remember, you can alter the statement or rewrite it to accommodate the comedy rhythm of your punchline.

HERE'S WHAT THIS WORKOUT WILL DO FOR YOU

This workout will teach you to look more deeply into any topic and discover areas that may seem matter-of-fact, but which have undertones of humor. For example, I am writing this at about the time of Hirohito's funeral in Japan. Jay Leno did the following joke about the funeral arrangements.

> "Security at the Emperor's funeral will cost $25 million dollars. How much security can he need? He's already dead."

You can see that the first line of that gag reads exactly the way it would in the newspaper. Leno's writers noted the inadvertent straight-line and provided the punchline.

HERE ARE SOME EXAMPLES

One line appeared in the newspaper before George Bush's 1989 inauguration. It stated that the President's new limousine cost $600,000. Here are some of the punchlines that resulted:

> . . . At that price, the President can rent out the White House and he and the family can live in the car.

★　　★　　★　　★　　★

> . . . It's a good thing he has the Secret Service accompany him everywhere he goes. You wouldn't want to leave a car like that in the hands of a parking lot attendant.

★　　★　　★　　★　　★

> . . . Of course, the President didn't pay cash. He just told the dealer to add it to the National Deficit.

★　　★　　★　　★　　★

. . . There's no word yet on how much Dan Quayle's moped cost.

★   ★   ★   ★   ★

. . . but the car comes equipped with everything—air conditioning, power steering and windows, a telephone, and a bumper sticker that reads, "I brake for Democrats."

A WORD BEFORE YOU START

You can see that all these ideas were a result of that one line of text in the newspaper account—"The President's new limousine will cost $600,000." It stimulated the mind to begin thinking. It was a factual, unfunny statement of fact, but it had tremendous humorous overtones.

There were other lines in the copy, too. For instance, the account noted that "the President could launch a nuclear attack from the back seat of this limo." That prompted the punchline: "George could try to roll down the window and accidentally start World War III."

You see the possibilities. Have fun with this one.

= WORKOUT 10B =
"Questions to Jokes"

This workout will be practice in reading between the lines. It gets you to go beyond the facts, to manufacture new facts. It recommends that you fantasize about your topic—let it get a little bizarre.

You do that by asking "What if?" Actually, you ask more than "What if?" You ask anything and everything you can think of about the topic. Investigate its beginnings, and what will happen if you project it to its natural or unnatural limit.

HERE'S WHAT YOU DO FOR THIS WORKOUT

1. Select a current topic from the newspaper. It can be the same one you worked with in Workout 10A or it can be entirely different.

2. Read through the newspaper account, and then make a list of ten questions that you might ask. The questions can be reasonable or outlandish. You may ask, "How will this affect the person's spouse?" Or, "What would have happened if this occurred during the Neanderthal Age?"

The questions are important only in that they stimulate your mind to think funny and creatively.

3. As a result of your questioning write at least three jokes on your premise. Remember, that the question itself doesn't necessarily have to appear in your joke. It can, but it doesn't have to. It's a catalyst that gets the fun happening in your mind.

HERE'S WHAT THIS WORKOUT WILL DO FOR YOU

This workout proves that your premise is literally without limits. You can change the time frame, the era in which it happens, the people it happened to, the results, the history—you can change anything you want about the premise in order to extract fun from it.

This exercise adds another dimension to your comedy writing. It expands your references and adds a zaniness to your writing.

HERE ARE SOME EXAMPLES

I'll stick with the same premise from the last workout—George Bush's new $600,000 limousine.

I asked myself why he needed a new limo and came up with the line:

"They had to get rid of Ronald Reagan's old limousine. The fuel line was clogged with jelly beans."

I asked how you would care for and worry about a car that cost that much and got the line:

"The first person who puts a scratch in that car is going to be appointed Ambassador to Libya."

I wondered about other things that would be in that price range and came up with this observation:

"That's typical of American consumerism. We have a Presidential limousine that cost twice as much as the President."

And I wondered if the newly-elected President got involved in the purchase price of the car and got this line:

"George Bush doesn't care what the car cost, just so long as it comes with an 8-year warranty."

A WORD BEFORE YOU START

I think you can see how the questions generated ironic observations. It also got into the zany—a car with jelly beans in the fuel line, and someone being sent to Libya for a minor accident.

So allow your head to go wild with this workout and have some fun.

= WORKOUT 10C =
"Finding Joke Formulas"

This workout will familiarize you with the formula joke structure, and show you that it can lead to very sophisticated, classic punchlines.

There are many joke formulas and they vary from comedian to comedian. Steve Allen does this word formula joke quite often.

> "Here's something that really gets my goat . . . and you know how painful it can be when your goat's been gotten."

★　　★　　★　　★　　★

> "This will warm the cockles of your heart . . . and you know how uncomfortable you can be when you've got cold heart cockles."

Bob Hopes does definition formulas frequently.

> "I came over here in a jeep. You all know what a jeep is—it's a New York taxicab that's been drafted."

★　　★　　★　　★　　★

> "You all know who Phyllis Diller is. She's Dolly Parton after taxes."

There are reverse formula jokes:

> "This guy is so rich, when he writes a check, the bank bounces."

★　　★　　★　　★　　★

> "My mother-in-law is so ugly when she sees a mouse, the mouse jumps on the chair."

I just listed these jokes to show you that the formula is alive and well in comedy. And that doesn't mean it's old. Listen carefully to the newer comics. Even Robin Williams uses repeating patterns; almost everyone does. It's a matter of style—form. No one can do a lot of comedy without repeating patterns.

There are so many formulas that it's practically impossible to list them. Besides, which ones do you list? The ones Robin Williams does, or Steve Allen's favorites, or Bob Hope's standards?

This workout is designed to help you discover some of these formulas, and also learn which ones you prefer and can use in your own writing.

In this workout, we'll put your powers of observation and analyzation to work again.

HERE'S WHAT YOU DO FOR THIS WORKOUT

1. Review the jokes, quotes, and one-liners that you selected in Workouts 1A, 1B, and 1C. As you reread them be aware of repeating patterns. Jot down any form that you feel is a formula.

2. Continue your research from memory or further investigation until you compile a list of at least ten different formulas.

Save this list. We'll use it in future workouts.

HERE'S WHAT THIS WORKOUT WILL DO FOR YOU

This should illustrate that some of the jokes you liked well enough to include in your collection of favorites—some of the jokes that you consider classics—are really formula jokes.

That shouldn't lessen their value in any way. It should rather increase your appreciation of formula jokes.

Remember, again, it's not the formula that makes a joke weak or cliché. It's how you fill in the blanks.

HERE ARE SOME EXAMPLES

I've gone back to some of my examples from Chapter One and have uncovered these jokes:

"A cynic is a man who, when he smells flowers, looks around for a coffin."

★   ★   ★   ★   ★

"War is only a cowardly escape from the problems of peace."

★   ★   ★   ★   ★

"Your friend is a man who knows all about you and still likes you."

★   ★   ★   ★   ★

"What is a writer but a schmuck with an Underwood."

★   ★   ★   ★   ★

"What, after all, is a halo? It's only one more thing to keep clean."

Aren't these all "definition" jokes? Couldn't they all begin with the Bob Hope formula I listed earlier—"You know what a cynic is. That's a man who. . . ."

In searching out other formulas, I came up with these:

The series of three. ("With all the hijackings nowadays there are three ways to travel—first class, tourist, and prisoner.")

★   ★   ★   ★   ★

The comparison. ("The beach was beautiful—all sand and water. That reminds me a lot of my golf game.")

★   ★   ★   ★   ★

The "who do you think you are . . ." ("My wife likes to spend money that she doesn't have. Who does she think she is—the government?")

★   ★   ★   ★   ★

The initials. ("I work for NBC. NBC—that means 'Nobody But Cosby.' ")

★   ★   ★   ★   ★

The fractured quotation. ("He who laughs first, probably told the joke.")

A WORD BEFORE YOU START

There's a wealth of good material, inspiration, and education in finding and using comedy formulas. Have fun doing this research.

= WORKOUT 10D =
"Formulas to Jokes"

Now that you see the value of joke formulas, this workout will help you to put them to use.

HERE'S WHAT YOU DO FOR THIS WORKOUT

Write at least ten jokes using the joke formulas that you uncovered in Workout 10C. Don't write all of your jokes using the same formula, though. Use at least five different formulas.

HERE'S WHAT THIS WORKOUT WILL DO FOR YOU

You'll learn the value of joke formulas and how plugging different values into the "blanks" can generate exciting, creative, funny *new* humor.

HERE ARE SOME EXAMPLES

I've been giving examples of this type of comedy throughout this chapter. Now you come up with them.

A WORD BEFORE YOU START

Joke formulas are valuable, provided that you don't overuse any of them. Work with many different styles and use them sparingly. Otherwise your writing may tend to get predictable.

Have fun filling in the blanks.

Chapter Eleven

WORKING WITH EXAGGERATION AND DISTORTION

People laugh when they look at images of themselves in crazy mirrors in amusement park fun houses. The distorted reflection in the mirror shows them as short and squat, or lean and lanky, or squiggly and misshapen. As they change positions, the image changes. It's always fresh and new and always distorted. That's why it's funny.

Caricaturists make fun of prominent people by exaggerating one or two of their features. Prince Charles's ears are always larger than necessary in cartoons, Durante's schnozzola was immense, Bob Hope's ski-nose is always exaggerated. Outstanding features are overstated just enough to be ridiculous, but not enough to destroy recognizability.

Impressionists generate humor that same way. They magnify a person's speech idiosyncrasies so much that it becomes funny. We recognize the star, identify the speech pattern, and laugh at it.

A good deal of comedy is based on distortion and exaggeration. Consider this gag:

> "I have a friend who's very big. He wanted to go to the University of Michigan, but he didn't fit."

Taken literally, this guy is bigger than a university campus. That's an obvious distortion of his size. Consider the following:

> "This guy was always big. His birthday is July 17th, 18th, and 19th."

Here we have more of an exaggeration. The physical image is not as well defined as the "university" analogy, but requiring three days to get born would indicate a large child.

The fun house mirrors, the caricatures, and even the impressionists deal only with sight and sound. With verbal humor we can distort and exaggerate both the concrete and the abstract. We can distort a person's size or we can exaggerate an idea. For example:

> "I knew a man who was so cheap he had vinyl pockets sewn into his suits so he could steal soup."

That joke magnifies the abstract concept of "cheap."

All of this is valuable for the humor writer because it's an area to look to for comedy. In any given assignment, look for the salient points. Then make them stand out even more. Magnify and highlight them. Distort them out of shape. Tug, twist, and pull them into ridiculous, funny concepts—the same way crazy mirrors reflect wacky images of your body.

Distortion and exaggeration stimulate humor in two ways. First, they create a bizarre image that can be funny in itself. David Brenner does a line about his own nose:

"My nose is so big, when I was a kid I thought it was a third arm."

Second, distortion or exaggeration can lead our minds into humorous avenues that can generate other lines. For example:

"If our budget deficit keeps growing, by the year 2015 the Statue of Liberty will get rid of the torch and replace it with a tin cup and pencils."

In that line, exaggeration led the thought processes to the future, which generated the gag.

How far can you go with exaggeration and distortion? There is a limit. You must retain enough connection with the original for the concept to be recognized. If the crazy mirrors reflected only colors and unrecognizable shapes, they wouldn't be funny. They might be interesting, but not funny. The reflection—although horribly distorted—has to be recognized as you. In the same way, your topic has to be identified in your exaggeration.

However, the mind is very flexible when dealing with these ideas. To illustrate, let's do some variations on the "university" line from above:

"My friend visited me recently. He stayed at the local hotel. Rooms 516, 517, and 518."

★   ★   ★   ★   ★

"He had a terrible day at the beach. He came home with 14 harpoon wounds."

★   ★   ★   ★   ★

"One day he stood on the corner wearing a red, white, and blue shirt, and a man came up and threw a letter in his mouth."

Notice in this routine, how the man's size keeps changing. First he's the size of a university, then the size of three motel rooms. From there he changes to about the size of a whale, then to the size of a mailbox. The sizes and shapes differ, but the mind has no problem accepting them.

It's similar to the continuity of a dream. We can be on a bus that magically transforms to a yacht that then converts to a desert that then becomes the interior of a nightclub. All of this is impossible, but the dreaming mind continues with the story, never pausing to question the transitions, never stopping to ask how or why.

These workouts can be playful, fascinating, and challenging. They can also be very useful for uncovering humor in most situations. Have fun with them.

= WORKOUT 11A =
"Big and Small Improvisation"

This is an improvisational workout that is meant to teach you to see things differently than they are intended. You will become the crazy mirror, reflecting distorted, disproportionate images.

It's good practice in not seeing things for what they are, but for what they might be.

HERE'S WHAT YOU DO FOR THIS WORKOUT

1. Gather ten ordinary, commonplace household items. These can be practically anything—shoelaces, spoons, eggbeaters, paperweights, desk ornaments, ashtrays.

You don't have to assemble these items physically, but you should make a list. And they should be things that you can see and study to help stimulate your thinking.

2. Improvise at least three comedy lines about each item. The comedy should be based on a distorted image of each object. In other words, you should make it something much larger or much smaller than it actually is. A white, ceramic cereal bowl, for instance, could become a stadium where the AFL plays most of their games. The AFL being the "Ant Football League." Or it could be a "pastie" that fell off the Abominable Snow Woman when she was doing an erotic dance.

HERE'S WHAT THIS WORKOUT WILL DO FOR YOU

This workout will force you to view things with a different perspective. You'll begin to recognize that nothing is either large or small except in relation to something else. The ordinary-sized cereal bowl, for instance, became a huge football stadium when compared to ants, but a small "pastie" when related to the Abominable Snow Woman.

This manipulative process is also valuable to use with abstract ideas. For example, major problems like the national deficit can be reduced to trivia by the comic. Conversely, minor annoyances, such as a family member continually changing television channels with the remote control unit, can be exaggerated into an earthshaking catastrophe by an inventive comedian.

HERE ARE SOME EXAMPLES

Here are few of the items that I selected and just a couple of examples of what I transformed each one into:

1. Two ordinary glass ashtrays became:

   a) Contact lenses for a nearsighted King Kong

   b) Kareem Abdul-Jabbar's cuff links

2. A wooden popsicle stick became:

   a) Mickey Rooney's diving board

   b) A surfboard for Smurfs

3. A wooden rolling pin became:

a) Tammy Bakker's make-up applicator

b) Leon Spinks's toothpick

A WORD BEFORE YOU START

You can readily see the distortion and the exaggeration that's necessary for this type of workout. You should see the fun, too. It wasn't mandatory that King Kong be nearsighted; it just seemed a little crazier.

Stick with this exercise; it will open up your thinking processes. By not limiting each item or each idea to its original concept, size, or shape, you create many new areas to explore for humor.

This workout should be fun.

= WORKOUT 11B =
"Bending Time and Space"

In this workout you'll find humor in distorting dimensions of time and space.

HERE'S WHAT YOU DO FOR THIS WORKOUT

Write at least three jokes on each of the following subjects:

  a) a very large living room
  b) a long wait for your spouse or date
  c) a statuesque lady with very long legs
  d) someone who wears a large hat size
  e) someone with a large nose
  f) someone with big ears
  g) someone with small feet
  h) slow service in a restaurant
  i) small hotel room
  j) a very heavy suitcase

HERE'S WHAT THIS WORKOUT WILL DO FOR YOU

This workout will show you how you can play with dimensions for comedic purposes. A room that is only slightly larger than average can be treated as immense. A time lapse of a few seconds can seem like eternity. The comedian can take these liberties and audiences will accept them.

This workout will train your mind to expand or shrink dimensions to suit the comedy.

HERE ARE SOME EXAMPLES

As an example, I've included a few jokes about a friend's new estate. Actually, it was a home that was larger than most, situated on a secluded piece of property. Since we were jealous, we had to make it seem like an obscenely wealthy estate.

Here's how we kidded "Charlie" about his "mansion."

"Charlie was involved in a five-car pile-up the other day. It wasn't serious, though. It happened in his own garage."

★　　★　　★　　★　　★

"Charlie's been out of town for a few days. He went to the front gate to pick up the mail."

★　　★　　★　　★　　★

"He installed little lights along the front walkway. The only problem is that planes from San Francisco keep landing on it."

★　　★　　★　　★　　★

"It's a beautiful home. Charlie and his wife not only have separate bathrooms, they have separate zip codes."

★   ★   ★   ★   ★

"It's a big house. Over the couch in the living room, there's a painting of Mt. Rushmore—actual size."

A WORD BEFORE YOU START

None of those jokes come close to the true dimensions. They all make the house and the property bigger than it actually is.

Of course, distortion can work in reverse, too, like the famous vaudeville jokes about how small the hotel rooms were.

"My room was so small the mice were hunchbacked."

★   ★   ★   ★   ★

"My room was so small I had to step outside to change my mind."

Allowing your thinking processes to toy with dimensions until they find the humor. This workout is a good exercise in expanding your mind.

Have fun working on it.

= WORKOUT 11C =
"Bending Abstract Ideas"

This workout is similar to 11B except that it deals with the exaggeration of abstract ideas.

HERE'S WHAT YOU DO FOR THIS WORKOUT

Write at least three jokes on each of the following premises:

a) how polite your date was

b) how mean your spouse is

c) how cheap your spouse is

d) how rough the nurse was to you

e) how poor your family was

f) how rough your neighborhood is

g) how much a fellow worker fawns over the boss

h) how lazy you (or someone else) can be

i) how dumb your friend is

j) how intelligent another friend is

HERE'S WHAT THIS WORKOUT WILL DO FOR YOU

The benefits of this workout are the same as for 11B, except that this one can be more of a challenge. Somehow physical dimensions seem easier to expand or shrink. Abstract ideas are more difficult.

HERE ARE SOME EXAMPLES

To illustrate this workout, I've selected the premise: "How conservative my hometown was." Here are some of the exaggerations:

"My hometown was so conservative, you had to have a prescription to buy a training bra."

★　　★　　★　　★　　★

"In the drugstore, *Reader's Digest* was sold in a plain brown wrapper."

★　　★　　★　　★　　★

"In the supermarket, breasts of chicken were labelled 'boobs of chicken.' "

★　　★　　★　　★　　★

". . . and in the display case, all the legs of lamb had to be crossed."

★　　★　　★　　★　　★

"When a tourist went into the drugstore to buy condoms, he had to describe them to the druggist."

A WORD BEFORE YOU START

Of course, none of these comments could ever be true, but you see how exaggeration can make a statement! This is an interesting way to let the mind expand on a concept, and it can generate some bizarre, wacky comedy.

It can often be the catalyst that brightens some otherwise factual, literal comedy. Have fun.

= WORKOUT 11D =
"Take It to the Limit"

In this workout you'll take a basically true premise and extend it to its ultimate conclusion. It may be a fact today, but sometime in the future it will be a joke.

HERE'S WHAT YOU DO FOR THIS WORKOUT

Write at least three jokes on each of the following premises. The jokes must be based on a glimpse into the future.

a) today's generation gap

b) the "greenhouse theory" (*scientists say that the earth is getting warmer*)

c) the pollution problem

d) salaries of athletes

e) the cost of housing

f) the skimpiness of bathing suits

g) poor workmanship

h) adult language in films

i) new technology (computers, fax machines, etc.)

j) sources of energy

HERE'S WHAT THIS WORKOUT WILL DO FOR YOU

This workout will add another perspective to your writing, another tool to your comedy workbox. It teaches you to accept today's premise, leave it intact, and find your exaggeration somewhere in the future.

HERE ARE SOME EXAMPLES

I selected growing traffic congestion as my premise:

"Traffic may eventually stop, everyone get out of their cars, pave over the whole mess, and start over again."

★ ★ ★ ★ ★

"Traffic may eventually get so bad that wealthy people will be born with a silver parking spot in their mouth."

★ ★ ★ ★ ★

"Traffic is getting so congested. Today you have trouble finding a parking spot. Someday you may have trouble finding a moving spot."

★ ★ ★ ★ ★

"Pretty soon you may not be able to pull onto a freeway until somebody dies and lets you have his place."

A WORD BEFORE YOU START

The future opens up possibilities for a whole lot of comedy. You can do whatever you want in the future, and who's to say it won't happen?

This workout should get your mind thinking in inventive, creative ways. This is like "science fiction" writing for humorists.

Have fun projecting humor into the future.

Chapter Twelve

WORKING WITH JOKE STRUCTURE

A joke is the basic building block of humor and it does have a structure—a form. The structure doesn't inhibit creativity because it permits variations within it. A house must have a structure, too. It must adhere to accepted building procedures, so that it will stand and be strong despite, wind, weather, and other variables. Yet within those codes, a house can be Colonial style or English Tudor; it can be one-story or two; it can be three bedrooms with a sunken den or five bedrooms with a Jacuzzi. The basic form allows unlimited originality.

Adhering to a structure enhances your writing without inhibiting you because it assures better jokes. The house that's built to code will stand longer and be stronger; so will your writing.

A house has a purpose. It is built to provide shelter from the elements—the wind, the rain, the cold. Therefore it must withstand those forces. As the three little pigs discovered, a house that blows down with the first strong wind is useless.

A joke has a purpose, too. The structure exists to help it fulfill its goal. Therefore, we can learn about joke construction by learning what a joke is expected to do.

The purpose of a joke is to amuse. It's similar to a skilled magician performing a trick. He pretends to do one thing while he unexpectedly does another. The magician tells us the red scarf is in his hand, but when we investigate we find a white scarf is there.

A joke is a verbal deception. It's a mental practical joke. The comedian outwits the audience, and they laugh in surprise.

The magic trick has two basic parts: what we think is going to happen—and what happens. Sometimes the magician tells us what will happen; other times we assume it. For instance, when a magic performer holds a cane in the air, he doesn't have to tell us it's a cane. We see that, and we *assume* it will always remain a cane. It doesn't. It magically and instantaneously becomes a bouquet of flowers.

The joke also has two basic parts: what we think is going to happen—and what happens. Or maybe it's better defined as what we *think* the comic means, and what the comic *actually* means.

Like the magic trick, what we think the comic means is often assumed. For example, Woody Allen once did a line about a writer friend of his who was busy "working on a non-fiction version of the Warren Report." The Warren Report contained the official findings of the Kennedy assassination. It was controversial at the time because people didn't feel it answered all the questions. So Allen's reference to a non-fiction version was funny, but only if people *assumed* the original was non-fiction, too.

The first thing a joke must do is provide information, or be certain that information is assumed by the audience. Unless a magician first convinces us that a red scarf is in his pocket, there's no surprise when a white scarf appears there. With the joke, as with our magical analogy, certain necessary information has to be provided.

We generally call that information the joke "setup." The setup is the first part of the structure and it has to accomplish three things:

1) provide enough information

2) not provide too much information

3) provide the correct information

Let's study each function separately.

1) PROVIDE ENOUGH INFORMATION:

In my speaking engagements I sometimes tell a story about my travels to Beirut with the Bob Hope television show. I travelled with the cast of the show to entertain the servicemen. That cast included Bob Hope, George Kirby, Vic Damone, Ann Jillian, Cathy Lee Crosby, Miss U.S.A., and Brooke Shields. You can understand that I wasn't the person that was usually mobbed.

On this trip we all wore white satin tennis jackets that the USO provided for cast and crew. It had a giant caricature of Bob Hope on the back and large writing that said, "Bob Hope Show—Beirut, Lebanon."

So one day, a crew member came over to me after the cast had left to do a non-televised show. He asked if he could have his picture taken with me. I was delighted until I found out he wanted me to turn around. All he wanted was the back of my jacket.

It's a cute, self-deprecating story that I enjoyed when it happened and enjoy re-telling. The audience usually enjoys it, too. But sometimes I forget to tell the listeners about the jacket that the USO provided. So when I tell them that the marine wanted a picture of my back, they don't know what I'm talking about. How could they? Consequently, there are no laughs. Why should they laugh? I haven't said anything amusing. It was the exact same story, told in the same way—except that I omitted an important ingredient.

To get people to think the way you want them to think, you have to be sure they have the necessary information.

2) NOT PROVIDE TOO MUCH INFORMATION:

This caution is important for two reasons. First, providing too much data can destroy the surprise. Let's go back to our magical analogy. The performer who says, "I have a red scarf in my hand," has told us enough. The white scarf then comes as a surprise. If the performer says, "I have a red scarf in my hand—well, it isn't necessarily red. There's a very good chance that it could be another color, like blue, or green, or —hey, how about white?" That performer has given us too much information. It detracts from the surprise.

The same thing applies with gags. You don't want to give so much data that you "tip" the punchline. You don't want the audience to see the joke coming.

Second, humor has a certain economy to it. The audience invests time listening to you. If they invest a little time and get a fair punchline, that's okay. If they invest a lot of time and get a great punchline, that's okay. But they don't want to listen for a long time and get a mediocre joke at the end. That gets groans instead of laughs. As a humorist, you protect your investment by being very economical with the setup. Don't dilly-dally with unnecessary words or information.

3) PROVIDE THE RIGHT INFORMATION:

As a humorist, you want to control the audience's thoughts. You want the listeners to be picturing some image in their minds; therefore, you have to give them the information that will paint that specific picture. Supply the wrong input, and you'll get the wrong result.

When I discuss this with writers in lectures, I tell about a friend I had in the very early grades in elementary school. This companion was a troublemaker, but a real charmer. We would both get into mischief that my good pal usually instigated, but I would suffer the consequences. My friend flashed that sunny personality and cherubic innocence and got off lightly every time. We went our separate ways eventually, but I still cherish that friendship and envy that bubbly, charismatic personality.

Then I ask the audience to paint a picture of this friend. Offer a description. In fact, why don't you do that briefly now? Put an image to the person I described in the last paragraph.

Most people paint a Huckleberry Finn type of character. Freckle-faced and red-headed are often included in the description. Very rarely does anyone guess that my good buddy was a little girl.

I sometimes use this story to illustrate how a humorist can direct an audience's mind in a certain direction. Here it shows you how essential it is that you provide the *correct* information

If you go back and reread that particular descriptive paragraph, you'll notice that there are no masculine or feminine pronouns. If I slipped up and said, "*He* always got me in trouble," that would certainly help the misdirection, but it would destroy the story. It could no longer be a girl. And of course, if I made a mistake and then corrected it—if I said, "*He* always, I mean *my friend* always. . . ."—I've tipped my hand. Everyone would know that I'm hiding the fact that she's a female.

Here's a story a client of mine used to tell that shows what I mean. He was reading some fictitious letters to "Dear Abby." One read:

> "Dear Abby, I'm 13 years old. I think I'm old enough to wear lipstick, rouge, and eye shadow. Yet every time my mother finds these, she throws them out and punishes me. Please write back and tell me who is right. Signed, Ralph."

The second part of the joke structure is the "punchline." It's the surprise. It's discovering a red scarf where we though there was a white scarf. It's called a punchline because it has to hit with the power of a punch. It has to be so sudden and unexpected that it almost knocks the wind out of the audience—figuratively, of course.

One way of accomplishing this is by saving the key words for the end of the joke. Consider these:

> Heavy drinker W. C. Fields said, "What contemptible scoundrel stole the cork from my lunch?"

★   ★   ★   ★   ★

He also said, "The cost of living has gone up another dollar a quart."

★　　★　　★　　★　　★

Here's a put-down that I've heard from many comedians. "He considers himself a legend in his own mind."

Notice that all of them are straightforward statements until the very last word. That's an ideal structure, but it's not always possible. It does, though, illustrate the effectiveness of holding the surprise as long as possible.

The economy of humor affects the punchline, too. It should remain crisp and uncluttered. Additional words and phrases often weaken the effect. In the W. C. FIelds example above, the word "lunch" is perfect. It's quick and effective. Changing it to "my bottle of lunch" or "my 100-proof lunch" would only diminish the effectiveness of the line.

These rules are flexible and subject to translation. One humorist may feel a few additional words help the punchline; another may feel they don't. That's the "seat-of-the-pants" nature of these guidelines.

Language may make a difference, too. Putting key words at the very end of the punchline may make it unwieldy. If it does, go with the natural rhythm of the joke rather than adhering to some regulation. Winston Churchill pointed up the silliness of following rigid rules for language when he scribbled on the margin of a document, "This is the sort of English up with which I will not put."

The joke structure needs to allow room for innovation and creativity. Creativity is supreme; rules, regulations, and structures are simply guidelines that help inspire originality and express it better.

= WORKOUT 12A =
"This Is My Life"

This workout is somewhat removed from humor writing, it is practice in the economy of words.

HERE'S WHAT YOU DO FOR THIS WORKOUT

1. Write an autobiographical sketch. Include some historical background, but make it primarily a sales pitch in which you try to sell a comedian, a producer, or an editor on your humorous writing. Don't be bashful; sell your good qualities. Make it at least a page and a half to two pages of double-spaced typing.

For now, that's all you have do with this workout. Let's move on to the others and we'll come back to discuss this one later.

= WORKOUT 12B =
"From Page to Stage"

This workout is an exercise in using the joke structure for writing the spoken joke.

HERE'S WHAT YOU DO FOR THIS WORKOUT

1. Collect six jokes from magazines, joke books, newspapers, or other publications. The jokes can be on any subject and should be gags that you personally enjoy.

2. Convert these jokes to conversation. Try to make them as effective as spoken jokes as they were as written jokes.

HERE'S WHAT THIS WORKOUT WILL DO FOR YOU

You'll develop your ear for comedy. You'll learn that what is written for publication is often too literary for spoken presentation.

You'll also discover that the published form usually has to be longer. It needs more description and explanation because it doesn't have the voice to add inflection. A comedian on stage can say the words "Thank you" in an unmistakably sarcastic tone. On the page, the words "Thank you" always seem pleasant unless qualified.

HERE ARE SOME EXAMPLES

Here's a joke as it might be published:

Two of my luncheon companions were razzing me one time about my thrift. I was defending my frugality as a virtue. I said, "I'm quite proud of the fact that I take care of my money. Do you know I still have the first dollar I ever made?" One friend quickly added, "And also the arm of the man who handed it to you."

Here's the same joke as I might present it verbally.

"I'm actually kind of a thrifty guy. My friends call it 'stingy.' My wife says, 'I not only have the first dollar I ever made, but also the arm of the man who handed it to me.' "

This could also be rewritten to put the joke on the other guy.

"I have a friend who's really cheap. He not only has the first dollar he ever made, but also the arm of the man who handed it to him."

A WORD BEFORE YOU START

This workout will show how to boil down a joke to just the essentials for verbal presentation. In the rewrite above, the sentence, "My friends call it 'stingy' " was removed without hurting the gag at all. I liked keeping it in because I thought it was a secondary little joke along the way. Others might feel it detracts from the main punchline. A head writer I worked for had a plaque in his office that read, "There are very few good judges of comedy, and even they don't agree."

Have fun playing with these jokes.

= WORKOUT 12C =
"From Stage to Page"

This workout is the opposite of 12B. It's practice in writing jokes for publication.

HERE'S WHAT YOU DO FOR THIS WORKOUT

1. Collect six jokes that you've told or heard others tell. They should be stories that you've only heard, not read.
2. Convert each of these to a short, funny paragraph.

HERE'S WHAT THIS WORKOUT WILL DO FOR YOU

This workout is good practice in writing a more literate form of joke. However, the rules of structure still apply. Say all that you need to say for the reader to appreciate the comedy, but keep the joke concise. You'll learn that you have to do more for the reader with this form. You have to explain and describe more because you don't have facial expressions or vocal inflections to help get your point across.

HERE ARE SOME EXAMPLES

Here's a joke that a stand-up comedian might do:

> "I think television is much better than the newspaper—except, of course, you can't swat flies with it."

Here's how that might be converted to a brief, humorous item for publication:

> "Our family was trying to watch TV one evening as my husband and son were debating the merits of the television media as opposed to the daily newspaper. Dad favored TV.
>
> As he was listing the merits of television, a fly started buzzing around his nose. My son said, 'Dad, why don't you roll up the TV and swat him with it?' "

Of course, that's only one version. It could be much simpler. Consider this version:

> "Two gentlemen were discussing television news as opposed to newspaper reporting. One said, 'What possible advantage does the newspaper have over television? '
>
> The other replied, 'You can swat flies with it.' "

A WORD BEFORE YOU START

These two workouts, 12B and 12C, highlight the difference between spoken and written humor. Each example could be redone by a different person and would come out differently. Yet the structure would remain intact. Notice, though, that in all the examples, the punchline comes toward the end. It speaks for itself because a good punchline doesn't need embellishment.

Any joke that ends with "You had to be there" or some such line, is not a joke at all. It's a plea.

Have fun with this exercise.

= WORKOUT 12D =
"Play With the Way You Say It"

Here you'll experiment with joke structures and rewriting gags.

HERE'S WHAT YOU DO FOR THIS WORKOUT

1. Gather six jokes from the personal favorites you've collected in previous workouts.

2. Make several attempts to restructure or rewrite each joke. Change the phrasing or the arrangement, add or delete words. Honestly try to improve the joke even though you already consider it a near classic.

3. Study the variations you've written and analyze them, comparing them with the original. If you think one of your rewrites is better than the original, find out why. If the original jokes remains best, discover why it tops your rewrites.

HERE'S WHAT THIS WORKOUT WILL DO FOR YOU

This workout may surprise you. Some of the work you do may turn out to be comparable or even better than the original. This workout proves that there are many different ways to write a gag.

You'll begin to see through your analysis why a joke has power. You'll begin to appreciate not only the basic joke idea, but also the way it is presented.

HERE ARE SOME EXAMPLES

I've chosen a real classic for my rewrites. It's Henny Youngman's line: "Take my wife—please." Here are a few variations I've tried:

1) "Now take my wife. Hey, There's an idea! Somebody please take my wife?"

★　　★　　★　　★　　★

2) "Take my wife—I'm begging you."

★　　★　　★　　★　　★

3) "Take my wife—*please* take my wife."

★　　★　　★　　★　　★

4) "Take my wife—anybody."

★　　★　　★　　★　　★

5) "Take my wife. In fact, you don't have to take her. I'll give her to you."

The first one's wordy. It doesn't have the impact of Youngman's version. The second version is good, but for another comedian. Henny Youngman's speech style is so clipped that the shorter version is better for him. But the rewrite isn't bad. The third is almost the same as the original. The few added words, though, don't really improve it. The fourth is a complete change of thought. It's not bad. The fifth is a new joke, too. It's not a Henny Youngman line, but it might fit a comedian who has a different style.

A WORD BEFORE YOU START

This experiment is interesting because the original line is so concise that it seems hard to tamper with, yet changes can be made.

Have fun trying to improve your favorites.

= WORKOUT 12E =
"This Is My Life—Again"

This workout is the completion of Workout 12A. It is separated from the first part of the workout so that you wouldn't read on and write with the second part in mind.

This is practice in the economy of words, which can be important in joke writing.

HERE'S WHAT YOU DO FOR THIS WORKOUT

1. Gather six jokes from personal favorites you've collected in previous workouts.

2. Make several attempts to restructure or rewrite each joke. Change the phrasing or the arrangement, add or delete words. Honestly try to improve the joke even though you already consider it a near classic.

3. Study the variations you've written and analyze them, comparing them with the original. If you think one of your rewrites is better than the original, find out why. If the original jokes remains best, discover why it tops your rewrites.

HERE'S WHAT THIS WORKOUT WILL DO FOR YOU

If you do this workout carefully, you'll be surprised at how much editing you do. Most of us "pad" our writing. We add words for flair more than clarity. We use words that don't say anything—that just look good on paper.

This workout may be gruelling, but it will also be enlightening. Economy is such an important part of humor that this workout is a valuable lesson.

HERE ARE SOME EXAMPLES

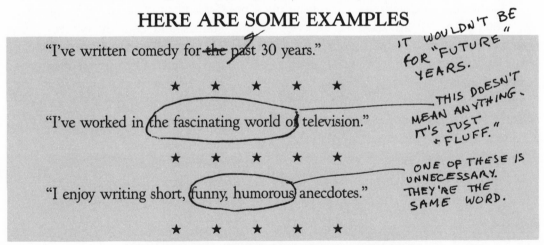

"I've written comedy for ~~the past~~ 30 years."

IT WOULDN'T BE FOR "FUTURE" YEARS.

★   ★   ★   ★   ★

"I've worked in (the fascinating world of) television."

THIS DOESN'T MEAN ANYTHING. IT'S JUST "FLUFF."

★   ★   ★   ★   ★

"I enjoy writing short, (funny, humorous) anecdotes."

ONE OF THESE IS UNNECESSARY. THEY'RE THE SAME WORD.

★   ★   ★   ★   ★

A WORD BEFORE YOU START

You get the idea. Especially be on the lookout for meaningless adjectives. Every mountain is majestic; every wolf's howl is mournful. Some writers say to cross out every adjective. That might be excessive, but it's a warning. Watch out for them!

As a matter of fact, we often use unnecessary introductory phrases, such as "as a matter of fact." They can go.

Don't misunderstand this workout, though. It is not meant to inspire you to write your humor in this way. Often introductory phrases help the comedy rhythm, and many times colorful adjectives do improve your writing. This workout is simply to make you aware of the words you use. Have fun doing it.

Chapter Thirteen

WORKING WITH SWITCHING

Have you ever retraced the pattern and flow of social conversation? It's like the flight of an inflated balloon that's released to zig-zag noisily around in the air. It seems random and chaotic, yet there's a physical reason for every twist and turn.

Conversation can be just as unpredictable as the balloon's flight pattern. Yet, there is a logic to it. One person talks about the ride over and how much trouble he had finding the Washington Street exit. "Washington" reminds another person of his vacation to the nation's capital. That prompts someone else to talk about a recent vote in Congress. Mentioning politics inspires another person to tell how her cousin's sister's son is working for a senator in Idaho. Idaho reminds someone to talk about this new recipe for potato pie that he got from his Aunt Tilly. The word "Tilly" gets someone thinking about tilling and she becomes philosophical about the plight of the farmer. Farming reminds another of a hayride she took as a young student.

The conversation shoots off in unforeseen tangents all born of the same circle.

That's what joke switching is—building a new joke from the basic elements of a previous joke. It's an accepted practice among comics and comedy writers. My partner and I once wrote a sketch for *The Carol Burnett Show* based on a slightly blue joke. The sketch worked beautifully and many people talked about it after it aired. A comedian I was working for mentioned that he saw it and enjoyed it. He immediately followed that praise with the comment: "Do you know the original joke?" He recognized the original gag that sired the sketch.

Here are four ways to switch a joke:

1) switch the setup   3) parallel the joke

2) switch the punchline   4) build on the inspiration

Let's look at each method in turn.

1) SWITCH THE SETUP:

With this switch, you keep the punchline intact and alter the buildup to suit your needs. This can be a method of personalizing stories to an audience. A joke that applies to bankers can often be adjusted to apply to bakers. A line about butchers might be switched to candlestick makers.

Here's a very simple idea of how to make a switch. A comedian, appearing before a convention of bankers, might say, "Bankers are notoriously cheap. Mr. Wilson called me three times to see if I would appear here tonight. I finally agreed to accept the charges."

You can see that the same line works if Mr. Wilson happens to be the program chairman for a group of bakers instead of bankers.

2) SWITCH THE PUNCHLINE:

Here it's the punchline that changes with basically the same setup. You've all heard some variation of the panhandler joke:

"Buddy, can you spare $5.00 for a cup of coffee?"
"Why do you need $5.00 for coffee?"
"Can I help it if I'm a heavy tipper?"

That might be switched to:

"Buddy, can you spare $2,000 for a cup of coffee?"
"$2000! Why do you need $2,000 for a cup of coffee?"
"I want to drink it in Paris."

3) PARALLEL THE JOKE:

With this method, you switch both the setup and the punchline:

"I bought this toupee very cheaply. The only problem is every time I pass a fire hydrant, one corner of it lifts up in the air."

That joke might be changed to:

"I think my wife knows the fur coat I bought her is a cheap imitation. Every time she wears it in public, it chases cats down the street."

Both gags are based on cheap animal fur replacing more expensive material, and the results. However, in the first one the setup uses a toupee and the dog pauses at fire hydrants. In the second, the setup is a fur coat and the dog chases cats.

These are two completely different jokes based on the same humorous idea.

4) BUILD ON THE INSPIRATION:

This is a generous interpretation of a switch. There's almost no logical explanation for the thought process. However, it does happen occasionally, so I'll list it here.

Let's get back to our analogy of the rambling conversation. Washington Street triggered Washington D.C. D.C. reminded someone of politics. Those associations are logical and understandable. Sometimes, though, thoughts pop into our heads that aren't logical. An airplane story could remind you of fruit salad. You don't know why it happens, but it happens.

The same phenomenon may occur when you're writing jokes. If it does, go with the flow. Profit from the inspiration.

It's difficult to illustrate this method because it's so capricious, but I'll try. Let's suppose the original jokes was about how old commercial planes are getting. It reads:

"Planes are getting so old now they fly on a mixture of jet fuel and prune juice."

For some reason—maybe that Ronald Reagan flies around to his speaking engagements, or maybe the prune juice reminded you of Reagan's age—it brings to your mind the fact that he gets $50,000 a speech. That motivates you to compose this line:

"Reagan now gets $50,000 for after-dinner speaking. That's a nice way to get a free lunch and a small fortune all at the same time, isn't it?"

Switching is also a valuable formula for improving jokes. In other words, if you have a joke that comes close but doesn't quite get the laughter you expect from an audience, try switching it. You might just come up with a real gem.

= WORKOUT 13A =
"Switch the Straight-Line"

In this workout we'll try creating new jokes while retaining the same punchline or, at least, the same punchline idea.

HERE'S WHAT YOU DO FOR THIS WORKOUT

Create five different buildups for the punchlines in the following stories. Use the same punchline or a recognizable equivalent. The punchlines are underlined.

"Several show business friends were out on a fishing trip when they were surrounded by a school of sharks. One of the theatrical agents fell overboard. The people on the boat watched helplessly as the sharks approached the terrified agent. Suddenly the sharks turned and swam away. One actor said, 'It's a miracle!' Another agent said, 'No. <u>It's just professional courtesy.</u>' "

★　　★　　★　　★　　★

"Ronald Reagan is one politician who doesn't lie, cheat, or steal. <u>He's always had an agent do that for him.</u>"

★　　★　　★　　★　　★

"One factory supervisor—the meanest boss in the whole plant—died suddenly. He had no friends, yet people turned out in droves for his funeral. One worker couldn't understand it. He said to his companion, 'How can he get this many people to show up at his funeral?' His buddy replied, 'It just goes to show you— <u>give the people what they want . . .</u>' "

HERE'S WHAT THIS WORKOUT WILL DO FOR YOU

It shows you that one humorous idea can have several different applications.

HERE ARE SOME EXAMPLES

Here's a punchline that I've found useful in speaking to various companies and associations. Basically, it's one joke, but with countless applications.

"I've spoken to many groups of salesmen. I've never faced an audience of salespeople that was not intelligent, bright, intuitive, and highly motivated . . . until tonight."

★　　★　　★　　★　　★

"I've travelled a great many miles to be with you people tonight. But with all the troubles that I experience in travelling, once I reach the stage and look out at the smiling faces, I'm always glad I came. I've never once had second thoughts . . . until tonight."

A WORD BEFORE YOU START

Obviously, that joke could be switched from salesmen to computer experts to hospital employees. But it can also be changed in other ways. How intelligent they look, how welcome they made you feel, how they look superior to you or how you look superior to them. The joke is the switch—"until tonight." Have fun with this workout.

WORKOUT 13B
"Switch the Punchline"

This workout is practice in changing the punchline. You often see this done if you watch *The Johnny Carson Show*. Johnny says, "It was so cold out there today that . . ." The new punchline—the switch—follows.

Practically every comic does a variation of this.

HERE'S WHAT YOU DO FOR THIS WORKOUT

Write at least ten punchline variations on each of the following three jokes:

"A panhandler came up to me on the street today and said, 'Hey buddy, can you give me $27.50 for a cup of coffee?' I said, 'Why do you need $27.50?' He said, 'I hate the taste of coffee, so I want to wash it down with a quart of scotch.' "

★　★　★　★　★

"A rabbi and a priest were seated in adjoining seats on a plane. The stewardess served the priest his dinner—baked ham. The rabbi said, 'I'd rather commit adultery than eat ham.' The priest said, 'I didn't realize we had a choice.' "

★　★　★　★　★

"I visited my friend in the hospital and the guy in the next bed was completely wrapped in bandages from head to foot. The only thing that wasn't completely wrapped in bandages was his right eye. Then the doctor came in, stood by his bed and said, 'I don't like the looks of that eye.' "

Note: Remember that you can change the setup slightly to accommodate any change you make in the punchline. For example, in the third joke above, instead of a doctor standing by the bed, it can be a nurse, or a friend, or even a burglar, if you like.

HERE ARE SOME EXAMPLES

"You know, they say that the family pet can often warn you when an earthquake is about to hit. That's true because we had an earthquake at six o'clock this morning, and last night my Irish setter took the family car and drove to Arizona."

★　★　★　★　★

"*(Same setup)* That's true, because last night my cat converted to Catholicism."

★　★　★　★　★

"*(Same setup)* That's true, because last night my goldfish hired some workmen to put a lid on their bowl."

A WORD BEFORE YOU START

You notice that most of the jokes are basically the same—switches on the original line. Some may be improvements, others may not. But if I write ten, the eighth one may be the gem. If three of them are gems, I could do them as a series of variations, building to the strongest one. By switching punchlines, you can search out your strongest joke.

Have fun playing with this workout.

= WORKOUT 13C =
"Parallel the Joke"

This workout is a combination of the previous two. It's a switch on both the setup and the punchline. The result is usually a joke that parallels the original.

HERE'S WHAT YOU DO FOR THIS WORKOUT

Write at least five new jokes that parallel each of the following:

"A friend of mine spent $500 dollars to go to karate class to learn how to defend himself. But it didn't work. So now he just pays the teacher to walk him home at night."

★   ★   ★   ★   ★

"My wife and I had an argument. She wanted to buy a fur coat and I wanted to get a new car. So we compromised. We bought the fur coat, but we keep it in the garage."

★   ★   ★   ★   ★

"My uncle's a great inventor. He just crossed a gorilla with a mink. It makes beautiful fur coats, but all the sleeves have to be shortened."

HERE ARE SOME EXAMPLES

Here are a few parallel switches on "How big my mother-in-law is." They are variations on the form, 'When she wore a white dress . . .':

"She wore a white dress one time and a bunch of kids thought she was the Good Humor truck."

★   ★   ★   ★   ★

"She wore a yellow dress one time and Big Bird got fresh with her."

★   ★   ★   ★   ★

"One time she wore a green dress with white stripes and two college teams played football on her."

★   ★   ★   ★   ★

"She wore a black dress once and threw the scientific world into turmoil. They thought it was an eclipse of the sun."

Those are all basically the same joke, but paralleling can also create entirely new jokes. Here's an example:

Original Joke:

"Do you like my ring? My grandmother gave this to me on her deathbed. She gave me $500 and said, 'Get a nice stone.' "

★   ★   ★   ★   ★

Changing both elements:

"I'm a very independent man today because of something my father said to me when I was a child. He said, 'Get the hell out of my house and don't come back.' "

★   ★   ★   ★   ★

Or:

I left my job today because of something my boss said to me. He said, 'You're fired.' "

A WORD BEFORE YOU START

Not all the switches you write will be better than the original. That's all right, though. At least you're experimenting. You're looking for a better joke. Often you'll find it.

Also, remember that not all switches have to be better; they simply have to be different. A joke that can't be used "as is" in a given situation, might be usable if it's switched.

Have fun with this workout.

= WORKOUT 13D =
"Switching New Jokes from Old"

This workout will be practice in using the switching formulas we've learned. You'll decide which method to use and how to use it.

HERE'S WHAT YOU DO FOR THIS WORKOUT

1. Gather ten jokes from your selection of your favorites.
2. Do at least three switches on each joke you've selected.

HERE'S WHAT THIS WORKOUT WILL DO FOR YOU

You'll be learning how to put the lessons of this chapter to work on good basic gags.

HERE ARE SOME EXAMPLES

I've picked one of the jokes from my selection and have done switches on it. I tried to illustrate this workout by doing one of each type of switch. You needn't do this, though. Just relax and have fun doing any style that pops into your mind.

The Original Joke:
"Be careful about reading health books. You may die of a misprint."

★　★　★　★　★

Switching the Setup:
"My uncle learned how to survive in the wilderness by reading a book about it. He poisoned himself on a misprint."

★　★　★　★　★

Switching the Punchline:
"Be careful about reading health books. A torn page could take five years off your life."

★　★　★　★　★

Paralleling:
"My uncle tried to become a champion diver from reading a book on the subject. It killed him. Somebody tore out the chapter about filling the pool."

A WORD BEFORE YOU START

Switching can generate lines that are related to the original but very different from them. It's a functional form of joke writing. The original setup and punchline give you a form to follow in writing your new version. They also focus your thinking, which always helps in comedy writing. They concentrate your mind on one form of joke, and prompt you to search out variations on that form. That focus stimulates the creative process.

Have fun practising it with this workout.

Chapter Fourteen

WORKING WITH JOKE BUILDING

I once told a story at a convention of story-tellers. The joke went over very well, and as I walked through the corridors of the convention hotel, I heard it repeated several times. No two speakers told the story the same way and none of them phrased the punchline exactly the way I did. Every one of these humorists "potchkeyed" with the story. "Potchkey" is comedy writers' slang for playing around with a joke.

This chapter is about "potchkeying" or joke building. It means to play with the joke, alter it, add on to it, refurnish it, redecorate it. It can even mean building a whole new joke.

Every joke that has ever been created can be the springboard for a better joke or a different joke. There's an old cowboy saying that goes, "There's never been a horse that couldn't be rode, and never been a man that couldn't be throwed." There's also never been a joke that couldn't be "potchkeyed" with.

These workouts will encourage you to experiment with jokes. They will get you involved in a kind of playful rewriting—a stream of consciousness, random, free association kind of rewriting. It's like the Rorschach test of comedy. When you hear a punchline, you recite the next few punchlines that come into your head.

Joke building has one purpose and that is to give the joke that pops out of your head (or anyone else's head) a second chance. You ad-lib an improvement. Well, it may not be an improvement. The original may be better. That's all right.

Joke building is improvisation. You create a joke or you hear a joke that someone else has created and you improvise a new form for it. You do it quickly and then select the best of the bunch. That becomes your joke.

The advantage is that instead of just one joke, you now have the pick of the litter.

In writing prose, you sometimes go through this process automatically. Let's suppose, for example, that you're writing a detective novel. You describe the lovely young girl who comes into your office. You say: "The door opened and a gorgeous blonde entered." No, let's make it, "an enticing blonde entered." Better yet, "a sensuous blonde entered." How about, "a long-legged, sexy blonde entered." You pick the best adjective and get on with your writing.

We do the same with a joke. We write: "This guy was so tough he used rope for dental floss." How about bailing wire for dental floss? If we really want to make him tough, "barbed wire for dental floss." How about, "He cleans his teeth by chewing on a grenade"? We might even say, "He uses a railroad spike for a toothpick."

That's the process. It's simple, it's unstructured, it's improvisational. Occasionally, though, it turns a pedestrian gag into a gem.

One final note. To a comedy writer, "potchkeying" is almost a compulsion. It's something you almost "cannot *not* do." You hear a joke and you have to try to make it better. Have fun.

= WORKOUT 14A =
"Potchkey"

This workout is practice in "potchkeying" with jokes. You will allow the jokes to roll around in your mind and change them in whatever way occurs to you. Some changes may be better, some may be worse. However, save that judgment until *after* you play with the gag.

HERE'S WHAT YOU DO FOR THIS WORKOUT

1. Review the jokes listed below. Some are good gags, some bad, some indifferent.

2. Take one gag at a time and allow yourself between five and ten minutes to "potchkey" with it. Come up with as many variations as you can by ad-libbing or improvising. If you come up with no variations, don't worry about it. Move on to the next. If you don't improve the gag, no problem. If you do feel your changes are improvements, note them and move on.

Here are the gags:

1. The White House is trying to cut government spending. At the last State Dinner they served hamburgers with the Presidential seal burned into them.

★　　★　　★　　★　　★

2. My husband is a klutz. He can't buy a hammer unless it comes with instructions.

★　　★　　★　　★　　★

3. My wife says she has nothing to wear, but if she bought it she wouldn't have any place to put it.

★　　★　　★　　★　　★

4. I know a guy who always cheats at golf. He once got a hole in one and wrote down a zero.

★　　★　　★　　★　　★

5. My uncle is such a bad driver. He considers a red light a recommendation.

★　　★　　★　　★　　★

6. My girl friend was so promiscuous, when she went to driving school, she spent the first two weeks learning to sit up.

★　　★　　★　　★　　★

7. Friends carried my husband home drunk so many times that they finally chipped in and bought him a suit with handles.

★　　★　　★　　★　　★

8. There's more than one way to skin a cat, and the cat's not crazy about any of them.

★　　★　　★　　★　　★

9. I have a friend who's so dumb he thinks Mount Rushmore is a natural formation.

★   ★   ★   ★   ★

10. My uncle hasn't touched alcohol in four months. He has a friend feed it to him.

★   ★   ★   ★   ★

11. My wife's such a bad cook I went in the kitchen the other day and caught a cockroach eating a Tums.

★   ★   ★   ★   ★

12. My uncle is so lazy, he never gets to the ballgame until the second inning. He wants to make sure he doesn't have to stand for the National Anthem.

★   ★   ★   ★   ★

13. My aunt is such a bad driver that people she drives by aren't called pedestrians; they're called survivors.

★   ★   ★   ★   ★

14. I didn't do badly gambling in Las Vegas. I went there in a $15,000 car and came home in a $200,000 bus.

★   ★   ★   ★   ★

15. My uncle invented a breath mint made from peanut butter. Your breath can't smell bad because it sticks to the roof of your mouth.

★   ★   ★   ★   ★

16. My uncle invented a new deodorant. You spray it on your body and you disappear. Then everyone stands around and wonders who smells.

★   ★   ★   ★   ★

17. I know a girl who is a real knockout. Men are just fighting to get a date with her. Unfortunately, they're fighting her husband.

★   ★   ★   ★   ★

18. I divorced my husband because of his bad memory. He kept forgetting he was married.

★   ★   ★   ★   ★

19. My children aren't bad kids. They're good kids who do bad things.

★   ★   ★   ★   ★

20. My parents had three children—one of each.

HERE'S WHAT THIS WORKOUT WILL DO FOR YOU

This workout will prove that no gag is carved in stone. Any one of these jokes can be improved or can lead to a completely different joke.

You will learn how valuable it can be to give your writing a quick second glance and take advantage of any improvements that might occur.

HERE ARE SOME EXAMPLES

"The freeway was so packed today, I was involved in a minor accident. Me and another car locked windshield wipers."

That's the original line. Here are a few of my improvisations:

". . . I smiled at another driver and we locked braces."

★　　★　　★　　★　　★

"locked sunglasses."

★　　★　　★　　★　　★

". . . I pushed in my cigarette lighter and set fire to the car in front of me."

★　　★　　★　　★　　★

"The freeway was really packed today. The woman in front of me kept shaking her head back and forth. Her ponytail was caught in my windshield wipers."

★　　★　　★　　★　　★

". . . Me and the car in front of me locked bumpers. Well, we didn't exactly lock bumpers. His got caught in my zipper."

★　　★　　★　　★　　★

". . . We were driving so close to one another, I hiccuped and swallowed the Garfield the Cat from the car in front of me."

A WORD BEFORE YOU START

I'll leave it to you to decide whether any of these are improvements. However, you see how one joke, coupled with just a few minutes of "potchkeying," can lead to variations, and perhaps new and better writing.

Have fun working on this.

= WORKOUT 14B =
"Write and Potchkey"

This workout is basically the same as Workout 14A except that you do it with jokes that you create instead of jokes written by others.

HERE'S WHAT YOU DO FOR THIS WORKOUT

1. Write at least five jokes on any topics you want.
2. Allow yourself from five to ten minutes to "potchkey" with them.
Have fun doing it.

Chapter Fifteen
WORKING WITH TOPPERS

Here's a story that a nightclub comic might tell:

> "You know, it's very sad, but I was just reading an article that said that one out of every four people in this world is mentally unbalanced. Yes, that's right—one out of every four is mentally unbalanced. Now if you want to see how true that is, here's what I want you to do. Think of three of your best friends."

> "Do they seem all right to you?"

> "Because if they do, then you're the one."

When a comedian tells that story in a nightclub, it generates three separate laughs. First, when the comic asks the people to think of three of their best friends, they look around the table at each other and laugh. Then "Do they seem all right to you?" gets another laugh on top of that one. Finally, the last laugh is on each one of them. It turns the table. They were looking at their friends; now they're the butt of the joke.

These are versions on the "topper." That's a joke built on top of another joke, an extension of it. Here's another example of the "topper:"

> "We were so poor when I was a kid, I used to wear trousers that were so worn that when I sat down on a quarter I could tell whether it was heads or tails.

> ". . . and whether George Washington had shaved that morning or not

> ". . . and whether or not he had his false teeth in."

The topper is an effective comedy device because it's so compact. It builds off a straight-line that's already been setup. Coming right after a laugh line, it catches the audience already laughing. It adds to the laughter, so it's a guaranteed "bigger" laugh.

It's also an economical comedy device because it cashes in two, three, or even more punchlines on only one straight-line. It's a comedy bargain.

Another effective variation on the topper is the comeback. That's where a joke goes in one direction and a topper, a variation on the same straight-line, is thrown back in the other direction. Someone does a line insulting you, and you turn it around.

> A husband says to his wife: "Honey, you would have made a great cook in the army. You make every meal taste like chipped beef on toast."

> She responds with: "Maybe that's because you make every day seem like World War II."

Toppers are valuable joke forms because they are practically a guaranteed laugh. They're worth whatever effort you have to expend to find them.

= WORKOUT 15A =
"Tuning In to Toppers"

A topper is any punchline that follows another punchline and utilizes the same straight-line. Many comics use them, but sometimes they happen so fast that we fail to notice them. This workout is going to help you to become aware of them.

HERE'S WHAT YOU DO FOR THIS WORKOUT

Collect at least ten examples of this form of comedy line. Listen for this type of joke on television. You'll hear plenty on sitcoms. Read magazines and joke books. Keep you eyes and ears ready to recognize the topper.

HERE'S WHAT THIS WORKOUT WILL DO FOR YOU

You'll appreciate the value of the topper when you hear it and you'll see that it does generate laughter when used properly.

Also, you'll discover that it is more common than you might have thought. It's used quite often in sitcoms. That's because it's a solid laugh producer, and it's also offers a fair distribution of comedy lines. One actor gets laugh #1, the other gets laugh #2.

HERE ARE SOME EXAMPLES

(From a nightclub comic)
"During the summer I made some money by playing in a dance band at a nudist colony. I was one of the lucky ones in the band. I played guitar.

". . . I know some of you guys in the audience could've gotten by with a ukulele.

". . . probably a few of you could have made do with a harmonica."

★   ★   ★   ★   ★

(From a nightclub comic)
"I hope you folks laugh at my jokes tonight. I laughed when you came in.

". . . I don't tell that joke when I work in a tough neighborhood."

". . . From the looks on some of your faces, I'm kind of sorry I told it here."

★   ★   ★   ★   ★

(From a speaker at a management association dinner)
"This is the first time I've ever addressed a management association. I hope I don't catch pneumonia. Before I came on stage, they made me remove my union suit.

". . . They were afraid I couldn't keep my trap shut."

A WORD BEFORE YOU START

It should be apparent that these jokes not only build on the same straight-line, but they should also build on laughs. The second one builds on the first, and the third builds on the second, in a natural progression.

Have fun searching out this form of humor.

= WORKOUT 15B =
"Topping the Tops"

Now that you know the form and have heard and seen it used often, this workout will get you to create a few toppers.

HERE'S WHAT YOU DO FOR THIS WORKOUT

1. Select five lines form your collection of favorites.
2. Write one or two toppers to each one of them.

HERE'S WHAT THIS WORKOUT WILL DO FOR YOU

This workout should teach you not to relax after a joke is written. It will be good practice in extracting even more humor from the situation.

Finding the workable topper may not always be easy, especially when you're beginning with well-crafted jokes. When you find the topper, though, you'll see that the results are well worth the struggle.

HERE ARE SOME EXAMPLES

I've worked up the audacity to try to add some toppers to the classic Will Rogers line that I listed in Workout 1A as one of my favorites. When asked what party he belonged to, Will Rogers said:

"I belong to no organized political party. I'm a Democrat."

(My *respectfully submitted toppers*)

"Democrat: that's like a Republican only with less votes."

★ ★ ★ ★ ★

"Our battle cry always seems to be 'wait till next time.' "

★ ★ ★ ★ ★

"The only thing we seem to have organized is our own confusion."

A WORD BEFORE YOU START

I'll readily admit that compared to the original these lines seem weak, but I will remind you to picture them in action. Hear Will Rogers speaking. If the first line generated good laughs, the follow-ups might have revitalized that laughter and kept it flowing even though they're not as strong as the original. That's the beauty of toppers.

This might be a challenging assignment, but it can be enlightening, too. Have fun with it.

= WORKOUT 15C =
"Write a Joke and Keep Going"

In this workout you'll create some comedy lines of your own that lend themselves to the topper formula—lines that can support a number of variations.

HERE'S WHAT YOU DO FOR THIS WORKOUT

Write ten comedy lines that have at least three punchlines. Choose any subjects you wish. The punchlines can be variations on the same theme, or additions to it.

HERE'S WHAT THIS WORKOUT WILL DO FOR YOU

This workout is good training in learning to extend a comedy idea beyond just one punchline. It's practice in extending the laugh and building onto it.

HERE ARE SOME EXAMPLES

This first is an example of variations on the same punchline:

"What's the difference between a liberal and a conservative? Liberals want to feed the entire world. Conservatives do, too. . . . but at a fund raising dinner.

★　　★　　★　　★　　★

". . . Liberals want equality for the whole world. Conservatives do, too. . . . but pro-rated by neighborhoods.

★　　★　　★　　★　　★

". . . Liberals want to spread out the wealth. Conservatives want to channel the wealth. . . . into campaign funds.

★　　★　　★　　★　　★

". . . Conservatives smoke a pipe. Liberals smoke anything they can get their hands on."

The next is an example of a punchline that keeps building:

"My wife is such a bad driver. She once got a ticket for parking on two roads at one time.

★　　★　　★　　★　　★

". . . It was Mr. and Mrs. Roads.

★　　★　　★　　★　　★

". . . They were in their kitchen at the time.

★　　★　　★　　★　　★

". . . There's a Ford in your future, but they didn't know there was going to be one in their dessert.

A WORD BEFORE YOU START

The first series of lines are all basically the same punchline. They can be interchanged without destroying the logic of the sequence. The second example is a progression. The lines build on each other. They can't be rearranged. Both forms build off the same straight-line, though, and both are acceptable. You might try a little of each in this workout.

Have fun with it.

= WORKOUT 15D =
"Taunts and Toppers"

In this workout you'll experiment with the comeback form of the topper. These are gags that build on the same straight-line, but reverse the direction of it.

HERE'S WHAT YOU DO FOR THIS WORKOUT

1. Write 10 insult jokes on any subject. They can be in dialogue form if you prefer.
2. Write a comeback so that the victim in the original 10 jokes can become the aggressor.

HERE'S WHAT THIS WORKOUT WILL DO FOR YOU

These are especially good forms for dialogue writing. In writing this type of comedy you get good training in not only doubling the laugh content, but also in balancing out the comedy lines.

HERE ARE SOME EXAMPLES

One gentleman kids another with: "That's a beautiful suit. Do you expect that style to come back?"

The other gentleman replies: "Why not? That joke did."

★　★　★　★　★

One gentleman says to a man with a beard: "You know I had a beard like yours once, but I did a very smart thing. I shaved it off."

The bearded gentleman replies: "I did a smart thing, too. I had a face like yours, so I grew a beard."

A WORD BEFORE YOU START

This is a nice form of comedy because it creates an underdog, then makes that underdog the victor. When the second line comes out, everyone is rooting for the speaker.

Have fun experimenting with these.

Chapter Sixteen

WORKING WITH REWRITING

Some say that all writing is rewriting. For many that's true; for others it isn't. It depends on your style of writing, your *modus operandi*. Some writers get their ideas onto paper with little thought about style; others think the writing process through thoroughly before touching the keyboard. Their rewriting becomes pre-writing.

However, all of us have to admit that at least some rewriting is required, even if it's only a quick glance through the pages to correct typos.

For the comedy writer, a quick read through is recommended because humor has a cadence, a rhythm to it that sometimes gets lost as we sit at the keyboard pondering, meditating, writing a little bit, then going back to pondering. The beat is interrupted. It's like a musician composing a melody piece by piece, playing part of it, jotting the notes on paper, thinking, playing, jotting. A song can't be appreciated that way. It has to be heard as one continuous flow.

Your writing, too, since it does have a comedy rhythm, has to be reread to feel the cadence.

Rewriting is worthwhile for the comedy writer—especially the beginning comedy writer—because it forces a little extra work on the project. One of the most glaring faults of novice humorists is quitting too soon. They abandon both the individual jokes and the overall project too rapidly. A quick rewrite affords you one last glance at the project before declaring it finished.

One caution, though. Humor has a spontaneity to it. It has an appeal based on the first hearing. It's a little like the woman who claimed she fell in love with a man at first sight. She fell out of love when she went back and took a second look.

Sometimes becoming too analytical about humor can destroy it. Looking too closely at the logic of comedy can ruin its spontaneity.

Rewriting that's unnecessary or too intense might improve the sentence structure, the grammar, or the logic of your piece, but decimate the comedy. The homespun philosophy applies to comedy writing: "If it ain't broke, don't fix it."

Most of your rewriting as a humor writer will be to do one thing—improve the humor content and get bigger laughs. Good grammar means nothing. Clever wording means nothing. Logic means nothing. Laughs mean everything. This doesn't mean that you can't improve the wording or correct faulty logic. It means that you shouldn't make improvements for the sake of improvements alone. You need to reword or correct the logic only if it helps the reader or the audience appreciate the humor more.

The workouts in this chapter deal mostly with rewriting the individual jokes. In the next chapter we'll discuss monologues, that is the blending of the jokes into a unified piece of material. That requires its own type of rewriting. For now, let's content ourselves with the process of improving the single gag.

Here are a few things to look out for in your final read through:

Most important, is it funny? If it is, you can go by it. You might try to improve it quickly as we saw in the previous chapter, or you can just be content with your work and move on. "If it ain't broke, don't fix it."

If it's not funny, find the reason why it isn't and do the necessary patchwork.

Some gags aren't funny because they're too direct. The joke is obvious and there's no surprise for the audience. The sentence is more a statement than a joke.

You rewrite this type of gag by hiding the joke element more. You imply it. You say what you mean by *not* saying it. The work you did in Chapters Four and Five would be a good review for this type of rewriting. It is substituting an image or a reference in place of a direct statement. The nightclub comic's comeback to a heckler is an example. "I'm surprised to see you here tonight. What are they doing? Cleaning your cage?"

That line doesn't say the heckler is an animal or is acting like an animal. It implies it. He must be an animal since he lives in a cage.

Some of your gags, though, may go too far in that direction. They may hide the joke so much that they become obscure. They may leave too many steps for the audience to fill in. For example: "You should see his girlfriend. He's late for every appointment he makes."

Where is the humor in that gag? Well, the author intended it to imply that his girl is so ugly her face could stop a clock. Okay, the reference is there and the humor might be there, but it's too much to ask of a reader or listener.

That joke needs a rewrite that would either explain the connection better or, at least, lead the audience further along so that they could more easily make the connection. For example: "His girl has a face that could stop a clock. He hasn't been on time for anything since he's been dating her."

Some of your jokes may need more graphic references. For example, you might say a man is "as nervous as a guy waiting to see his doctor." Well, that may explain the nervousness, but it doesn't really create a graphic, comic image. However, this line does: "He was as nervous as a long-tailed cat in a room full of rocking chairs."

Other references may be perfect for conveying the image you want, but they need more color, more "pizzazz." You could rewrite those by adding colorful phrases or images. For instance: "The sand was so hot that he walked across it like a tap-dancing chicken." That's not bad, but you might improve it with even more descriptive language. "The sand was so hot that he walked across it like a chicken tap-dancing to a record being played at the wrong speed."

Rewriting is a very individual art. Each of your jokes deserves one last look, but it may not *require* a revision. If the joke satisfies you, it's finished. If it doesn't, rework it. Just be wary of writing comedy into non-comedy. Your first reaction is usually correct.

= WORKOUT 16A =
"Mark and Make It Better"

In this workout you'll practice reading over your "finished" jokes, with a critical eye toward those that need a rewrite.

HERE'S WHAT YOU DO FOR THIS WORKOUT

1. Gather any 25 of your original jokes from previous workouts.
2. Read through the entire 25 and mark those that you feel might be improved with a rewrite.

Note: I know we recommended not being too critical in your evaluation. "If it ain't broke, don't fix it." However, for the purpose of this workout, you might select more of your jokes for a rewrite than you would otherwise. In other words, be a little harsher in your criticism, for the sake of practice, than you ordinarily would be.

3. Make a brief marginal note on why and how the joke you marked could use improvement.

HERE'S WHAT THIS WORKOUT WILL DO FOR YOU

This workout will teach you to take a final, honest, critical look at your work. It will teach you to view your work dispassionately, to see and hear it as an audience would, and to evaluate its effectiveness as honestly and accurately as you can.

HERE ARE SOME EXAMPLES

Here are a few lines about driving. I'll list them here and make marginal notations, just as you might do in this exercise.

"Let me give you folks an idea how I drive. Have you ever seen the movie *King Kong*? Well, put wheels on him and that's me.

    ★   ★   ★   ★   ★

MAYBE A MORE CURRENT REFERENCE THAN KING KONG.

"I once got a speeding ticket . . . in my own driveway.

    ★   ★   ★   ★   ★

TOO DIRECT AND NOT CLEAR ENOUGH.

"I got my driver's license by default. The officer gave it to me rather than get in the car with me.

    ★   ★   ★   ★   ★

TOO DIRECT NOT COLORFUL ENOUGH MORE GRAPHIC

"I don't know if I can park or not. Some policeman always makes me get out of the car before then.

NOT CLEAR. MORE GERANIC

★ ★ ★ ★ ★

"My father taught me how to drive years ago. . . . when I mentioned I was thinking about leaving home.

BETTER WORDING

★ ★ ★ ★ ★

"He skipped all the technical parts. He just got me to a steep hill and pushed.

GOOD COMIC IDEA BUT NOT WORDED FUNNY ENOUGH.

★ ★ ★ ★ ★

"My kids won't drive with me. They claim they're too young to die.

TOO DIRECT JUST A STATEMENT NEED BETTER REFERENCE

★ ★ ★ ★ ★

"I once got a $750 dollar fine for parking. I don't care what the officer says, I was there before the airplane was."

OR COULD BE CLEARER

★ ★ ★ ★ ★

A WORD BEFORE YOU START

Most of my comments are contained in the marginal notes. We'll be using this collection of example jokes as we go through the remaining workouts of this chapter.

You might read over the jokes in the example above and decide which ones *you* would rewrite and which *you* would leave as is—and note *your* reasons why.

Have fun with this workout.

= WORKOUT 16B =
"Redirect the Too Direct"

In this workout you'll get practice in hiding the joke more. You'll learn to say something by not saying it, but by implying it.

HERE'S WHAT YOU DO FOR THIS WORKOUT

1. From the list of jokes you made in Workout 16A, select those that you marked as too direct.

2. Briefly review Chapters Four and Five.

3. For each of these jokes, make a list of five things that would imply your reference rather than say it straight on.

HERE'S WHAT THIS WORKOUT WILL DO FOR YOU

The purpose of hiding the joke more is to keep the surprise fresh for the audience. That adds more punch to the punchline.

You'll probably use this rewriting technique more than any other in doing comedy, and you will find that it will help your humor tremendously.

HERE ARE SOME EXAMPLES

In Workout 16A, I marked several of my example jokes as too direct. One was:

"I once got a speeding ticket . . . in my own driveway."

It's not as funny as it could be. So here are a few other references that might say "bad places to drive fast:"

1) against traffic

2) inside your garage

3) on Times Square . . . on New Year's Eve

4) in an automobile showroom

5) in the kiddie rides at Disneyland

6) on an airport runway

From that list of references, I rewrote the line to hide the joke more. It now reads:

"I once got a speeding ticket for going just 25 miles an hour . . . down Times Square . . . on New Year's Eve."

Another joke that was too direct was:

"My kids won't drive with me. They claim they're too young to die."

Again, we need more references that say "die."

1) meet my maker

2) leave this world

3) that could be curtains

4) if it's the last thing I do

5) deader than a door nail

6) buying the farm

From that list, I settled on a variation of "leave this world," because it ties in with parenthood or "bringing someone into the world." I rewrote the joke as follows:

"My kids won't drive with me. They say they'll settle for just having me bring them *into* this world."

A WORD BEFORE YOU START

Both of these rewrites make the jokes a little more of a surprise. In the first one, there's a moment when the audience wonders why you'd get a ticket for driving at such a slow rate of speed, then you tell them it's New Year's Eve, when that street is packed with revelers. A car couldn't travel that road at one mile an hour.

The second one hides the joke nicely. It says that the kids don't want to leave this world, which is the natural result of driving with this person. But it says it without saying it. It makes the audience hunt for the punchline a little bit, making it more of a surprise.

Try to rework the jokes you marked as too direct in the same way. Have fun with it.

= WORKOUT 16C =
"Make It More Vivid"

In this workout you'll get some practice in finding more vivid references to rejuvenate your jokes.

HERE'S WHAT YOU DO FOR THIS WORKOUT

1. From the list of jokes you marked in Workout 16A, gather those you feel might be helped with a more graphic reference.

2. For each joke you selected make a list of at least seven different references.

3. Rewrite each of your jokes using at least one of the new references that you listed.

HERE'S WHAT THIS WORKOUT WILL DO FOR YOU

This exercise will help you to recognize and to correct those jokes that "come close, but win no cigar." Generally, they just lack a little "oomph," a little nudge that pushes them from the mediocre to the "pretty darn good," or even all the way into the "gem" category of gags.

That little nudge is often a more graphic, more vivid image—a better reference.

HERE ARE SOME EXAMPLES

The gags I've selected for a rewrite here are:

I got my driver's license by default. The officer gave it to me rather than get in the car with me.

★　　★　　★　　★　　★

I don't know if I can park or not. Some policeman always makes me get out of the car before then.

★　　★　　★　　★　　★

Basically, they're true statements. The idea is funny, but it just sits there. There's no punch to it. What each one needs is a more graphic image. More of a funny picture for the listener to create in his or her own mind.

So I tried to create some funnier images:

1) maybe the officer ran away

2) maybe he got in the car and just gave me the license so he could get out

3) maybe he got in the car and something terrible happened to him.

That last is the one I want. I want to create a mysterious image of this poor man who had to give me the driver's test. I rewrote the gag as follows:

"I got my driver's license by default. They never found the officer who gave me the test."

Again, I want a funnier image for why I have never learned to park. This gag says that some officer always pulls me over, but that's not graphic enough. It doesn't tell a funny enough story or create a funny image.

So I envisioned other reasons why I couldn't learn to park:

    1) I never learned how to stop the car

    2) I don't need to park because I'm always involved in an accident

    3) there's never enough left of the car I drive to park

That's the one. Every time I take a car out for a spin I totally destroy it. There's never anything left to park. The rewritten joke now reads:

"I don't know if I can park a car or not. I've never had a car last that long."

A WORD BEFORE YOU START

You can see how the more vivid image helped these gags. It painted a funny image in people's minds, and both of the suggestions were vague enough to allow the listeners to add some details of their own. It always helps, if it's not too obscure, to allow the listeners to write some of the joke, to fill in the blanks, as it were.

That's the kind of improvement you want to make by searching out more graphic images for your gags.

Have fun with this one.

= WORKOUT 16D =
"Add Some Lilt"

Sometimes your references are helped with a bit of razzle-dazzle, fancy footwork. In basketball it's called "dribbling behind the back." It's just a bit of showboating that might amuse your audience. That's what this workout will utilize.

HERE'S WHAT YOU DO FOR THIS WORKOUT

1. Use the same list of jokes that you used for workout 16C.

2. For each joke that you've selected, make a list of at least five colorfully descriptive words that could be added to your reference.

3. Rewrite your joke, sprucing it up with one or more of these descriptive words or phrases.

HERE'S WHAT THIS WORKOUT WILL DO FOR YOU

You might find that your joke and your reference are ideal, but the joke feels flat. It doesn't have the lilt, the cadence that it needs. It doesn't sound right. This exercise will teach you that adding syllables, colorful words, and a little rhythm to the gag can often improve it, maybe even save an otherwise worthless joke.

Note (of caution): Remember, not all jokes will be helped by adding words; some are improved, in fact, by cutting them. However, this workout provides practice in adding words to gags that need extra "oomph." Even though this isn't the answer to all gags, it's well worth devoting some practice writing time to it.

HERE ARE SOME EXAMPLES

I've selected these jokes for improvement:

"My father taught me how to drive years ago. . . . when I mentioned I was thinking about leaving home."

★　　★　　★　　★　　★

"He skipped all the technical parts. He just got me to a steep hill and pushed."

These jokes have the germ of a funny idea, but they lack rhythm. They're missing something. They need to become more whimsical and lyrical. I tried this:

"My father taught me how to drive years ago. I wanted to run away from home and he couldn't afford bus fare."

★　　★　　★　　★　　★

"He skipped all the technical parts. When we came to our first steep hill, he said, 'Write to Momma,' and jumped out."

That last joke prompted me to do a follow-up that adds an even more graphic picture. It goes:

"That car rolled for two hours before I finally came to a highway."

A WORD BEFORE YOU START

The lilt of those phrases—"couldn't afford bus fare" and "Write to Momma"—helps the gags. The lyrical wording helps paint a more vivid image, too.

Note that the ideas are basically the same; it's just the new wording that enlivens the jokes.

A fringe benefit that often happens, too, is the added gag that was tacked onto the second joke. This occurs frequently when you rewrite gags.

Try improving some of your joke writing with more colorful, picturesque language. Have fun with this workout.

Chapter Seventeen

WORKING WITH MONOLOGUES

"Monologue" is an awkward sounding word that defines a very pleasant comedic art form. It's the basis of most stand-up comedy, although it can take many forms. Steve Martin's style is different from Robin Williams's style, which is different from Rodney Dangerfield's style, which is different from Joan Rivers's style.

That's because each person is different. Each has a unique speech pattern, sense of humor, point of view, and delivery.

A stand-up comedy monologue is a deceptive art form, too. Done well, it appears almost effortless. Comedian Tom Dreesen says that a performer should have a "conversation" with an audience—not give a presentation. A presentation implies something that is choreographed, rigidly formatted. A monologue may be that. It may be written and presented without changing a comma. The comic may use the same gestures and the same voice inflection each time he performs it. However, the impression is that it is free-flowing, improvisational, "top-of-the-head" conversation.

The hard work put into the composition of the monologue and its delivery makes it look spontaneous.

A good monologue should have a structure, a form. Sometimes, the apparent lack of form can be the structure. For example, Henny Youngman used to get laughs at Friars' Roasts with his non sequiturs. He'd say, "Sure we're here to honor Milton Berle, but Milton Berle has a wife. But how 'bout my wife? My wife went to the doctor the other day. . . ." Then he'd continue on with his doctor joke.

That's a gimmick that works for him, and gimmicks are allowed in comedy. Generally, though the routine has a logical flow. It discusses one facet of the topic, then moves to another, then another. It might go on to blend smoothly into another topic, discuss one facet of it and then the next.

To hop around randomly, unless it's done for effect, can be disconcerting to listeners.

A comic monologue should have a point of view. Since it is conversational, the comic should have something to add to the discussion. Especially, since the comedian at the microphone is the one who brought up the topic in the first place.

If you're talking about gun control, are you for or against it? Do you agree with the NRA or are you firmly opposed to it? This doesn't imply that you have to preach— not at all. But your point of view should be consistent. It doesn't have to be right, but it should be constant.

If it's not, you confuse the audience. One time you're pro and the next instant you're con. They're not quite sure who they're listening to or what you're saying.

There are ways of expressing an opposing point of view. For example, you might preface a line by saying, "There are some people who think differently; they say . . ." and then continue with their point of view. So you can do jokes from both sides of the argument, but listeners should have a fairly good idea of where you stand.

They should also have a clear idea of who you are—or at least who your stage persona is. If, for example, your stage persona is supercilious, your monologue should be. If your stage character is pompous, your dialogue should be stilted.

Some comedians can be very witty, speaking with fancy vocabularies and precise enunciation. Will Rogers, though, used "ain't" as much as any other word, and spoke with his Oklahoma drawl. It sounded natural from him. It wouldn't from Peter Ustinov.

W. C. Fields loved overblown oratory. He might call someone a "contemptible scoundrel." Rodney Dangerfield might call the same person a "lousy bum."

Whoopi Goldberg in her comedy act, does many characters. They all speak differently, yet each one is consistent. If she's doing a Valley Girl, all of the speech sounds like a Valley Girl. If she's doing a street tough, she sounds menacing and uses street language. Consistency.

As a writer, you have to determine who is going to speak your words. Discover that speech pattern and stick with it. The words you use must sound as if they're coming from the speaker.

A monologue is obliged to be interesting. To get people to listen, you have to make them want to listen. You have to keep them listening, too. Monotony can kill the fun of a comedy routine.

You may have heard that some people are so naturally funny that they could be amusing reading the phone book. Well, they can't. Not unless they're doing something else to make it interesting.

In your writing, avoid the "phone book" or "laundry list" syndrome. Keep the conversation lively, energetic. Keep the listeners listening.

It should go without saying—but we'll say it anyway—that a comedy monologue should be comedic. It has to generate laughs. There's something the danger as a writer and as a performer that you get so caught up in what you're saying that you forget to be funny. Guard against it.

I listened to a routine of Whoopi Goldberg's in which she is a street tough visiting the attic where Anne Frank lived. It's a touching monologue. Whoopi has the audience near tears when she admits that the character is crying. Then her character says, "And I'm not the crying type. I'd as soon cut your throat as look at you."

Even in this poignant moment, Whoopi remembers to get laughs.

The following exercises will help you develop some of the skills you'll need to compose good, funny monologues.

= WORKOUT 17A =
"Plant Your Premise"

When you converse with an audience in monologue form, it's essential that they know what you're talking about. You have to establish a premise, define it, and offer your point of view. And you must do all that as economically as possible.

It's a good idea to establish the frame of reference with jokes wherever possible. That's what you'll be doing here.

HERE'S WHAT YOU DO FOR THIS WORKOUT

1. Create five topics that you would like to write monologues on.
2. For each topic, establish your premise. Let your audience know as much about your outlook on it as possible by writing three appropriate opening jokes. These jokes should be funny, but primarily they should lay the groundwork for the monologue material to follow.

HERE'S WHAT THIS WORKOUT WILL DO FOR YOU

This will be practice in establishing common ground for your "conversation" with the audience. You want to be very explicit. The audience needs to know exactly what your premise is and how you feel about it.

One producer I used to work for would say, when we had differences of opinion, "I don't want you to necessarily agree with me; I just want to be sure you *understand* what I'm saying." That's how you should learn to be with your audience.

It needs to know exactly what you're saying so that it can appreciate the humor of what you're saying.

HERE ARE SOME EXAMPLES

"My mother always believed that cleanliness was next to Godliness. When I was a kid, she used to keep me and my brothers so clean we thought we were for sale."

★ ★ ★ ★ ★

"And 'clean' to my mother meant 'starch.' She starched everything. One time I sneezed and cut my nose on the handkerchief."

★ ★ ★ ★ ★

"We hated it because she starched everything. My brother fell out of bed one night and broke his pajamas."

A WORD BEFORE YOU START

It should be apparent from these gags that my premise is Mom's cleanliness. What did we think about it? Naturally, we hated it. Kids don't like being too clean. We especially hated the starch because it made everything feel uncomfortable.

This premise can lead to all sorts of material, but I think these lines give you an idea of how to set the premise and establish your point of view quickly and naturally.

Have fun working on the premises in this workout.

= WORKOUT 17B =
"Add a Different Handle"

A monologue, since it is talking about one subject, can become repetitive. The writer has to guard against that by varying the form. In other words you can do the same type of jokes or gags on the same topic, but you need to change the phrasing.

This workout will be practice in writing jokes about the same idea, but varying them to keep the audience interested.

HERE'S WHAT YOU DO FOR THIS WORKOUT

1. Select any three of topics you created and worked on in Workout 17A.
2. Write seven jokes about each topic.
3. Vary the phrasing and presentation of each joke so that it fits logically into a natural flowing, conversational routine.

HERE'S WHAT THIS WORKOUT WILL DO FOR YOU

This is practice in using similar gags without letting them appear similar. For example, they shouldn't all read, "It was so cold out that . . .," even if, basically, they are all, "It was so cold out that . . ." jokes. You can brighten up the cadence with conversational introductory statements that add spice to each gag.

HERE ARE SOME EXAMPLES

As my example, I'll just continue with the "Clean Mom" jokes that I used to illustrate Workout 17A.

"That's why I became a stand-up comic. I couldn't sit down because my pants don't bend."

★   ★   ★   ★   ★

"And I mean Mom put lots of starch in our clothes. When I sweated my underarms turned blue."

★   ★   ★   ★   ★

"I broke my arm once and we saved a lot of money. The doctor said I could use my shirt as a cast."

★   ★   ★   ★   ★

"Mom starched things that people normally don't starch—like socks."

★   ★   ★   ★   ★

"The dog used to chew on my sock but only because she thought it was a bone."

★   ★   ★   ★   ★

"Here's how fanatical she was. Mom even put starch in our bath water. True. I had rigor mortis when I was seven years old."

A WORD BEFORE YOU START

Now these are all "My Mom used so much starch that . . . jokes." However, they make a nice, conversational chunk of a monologue because they're varied enough.

You may eventually drop some individual gags and add others, but as is, this makes a solid small 8- to 10-joke piece of a monologue.

You see how the addition of an introductory phrase seems to change the structure of the joke? It varies the pattern enough so that the formula is not readily detectable.

Notice, too, that if you set up the premise well you can eliminate introductory phrases. "That's why I became a stand-up comedian" doesn't mention starch at all. It's implied from the previous lines.

So add some variety to your monologues by toying with the wording of them. Keep it varied. Have some fun with this workout.

= WORKOUT 17C =
"Putting Your Ducks in a Row"

In this workout you'll practice putting an entire monologue together using your skills from Workout 17A and 17B.

You'll set up the premise of each subtopic and vary the phrasing to keep the monologue lively.

You'll also work on establishing a point of view and maintaining it.

HERE'S WHAT YOU DO FOR THIS WORKOUT

1. Go back to the 30 monologue jokes you wrote as your assignment in Workout 9D.

2. Arrange these jokes in a logical order. Put them in a form that is flowing, natural, and conversational.

3. Re-examine the foundation for each subtopic. If you haven't explained it well enough, write new jokes that will accomplish that.

4. Find inconsistent spots in your monologue—places where you say "black is black" in one joke and "black is white" in another—those places where you contradict your own point of view. Rewrite whatever gags you must to restore consistency to your point of view.

5. Read over your almost completed monologue. You may spot "holes" in it—that is, gaps in the logic, places where the dialogue doesn't blend, the conversation doesn't flow, the transitions are jarringly abrupt. Note them.

6. Repair those "holes." This may necessitate writing new jokes, changing existing jokes, of deleting jokes—whatever it takes to make the "conversation" flow naturally.

HERE'S WHAT THIS WORKOUT WILL DO FOR YOU

This workout is good training in constructing a workable monologue. It gives you practice blending a series of disconnected jokes into a routine that feels natural.

Through this workout you'll begin to get a feel for the pacing of a monologue. You will learn to hear it and experience it the way your audience might.

This will teach you not only to write the funniest material you can, but also to keep it fast-moving and interesting for the listeners.

HERE ARE SOME EXAMPLES

Look at the next workout. Meanwhile, have fun working on this one.

= WORKOUT 17D =
"Fixing the Finest"

Those of us who aspire to comedy careers are lucky. We have the greatest teachers in the world available to us on television, in clubs, and on records. This workout helps us take advantage of the teaching of the masters.

HERE'S WHAT YOU DO FOR THIS WORKOUT

1. Find an example of a good, professional monologue. Recordings of Bill Cosby, Jackie Mason, Whoopi Goldberg, and many other comics are excellent source material.

2. Select one appropriate recording of a monologue. Make a transcription of it.

3. Study that monologue on paper with the same critical eye that you devoted to the previous workouts in this chapter.

4. If you spot any areas that could use improvement, rewrite to make those corrections. If you don't see any areas that could be improved, fine. You'll still learn from this workout because you will have studied and analyzed a monologue that you consider perfectly formed.

HERE'S WHAT THIS WORKOUT WILL DO FOR YOU

You're studying a monologue that has probably been very successful. Otherwise, the performer is unlikely to have recorded it. You'll be able to see why this routine "clicked."

If you found areas that needed improvement and then worked to make the improvements, you learned that any piece of material, regardless of how successful, can be rewritten.

The rewrites may simply be changes to adjust that monologue to your style. That, too, is a valuable writing lesson.

HERE ARE SOME EXAMPLES

Here is a brief section of monologue that I borrowed from a speaker who addressed a group of hospital workers, along with some of my notes:

I just got out of the hospital. Everything was all right though. I wore clean underwear and everything.

★   ★   ★   ★   ★

I had heart surgery. In fact, the doctor who did my surgery is at this banquet tonight. His wife is cutting his meat for him.

★   ★   ★   ★   ★

I had to go to Cardiac Rehabilitation classes three times a week. It was difficult because it came at a time in my life when it was hard of me to do anything three times a week.

★   ★   ★   ★   ★

The head nurse of this department was known as the "Mr. T of RNs."

★   ★   ★   ★   ★

She had a black belt in nursing.

★   ★   ★   ★   ★

If I ever need a heart transplant, I want to get one from one of the folks who work in Cardiac Rehab. I want to get one that hasn't been used before.

★   ★   ★   ★   ★

We used to ride the stationary bike for a full half hour. This one guy was screaming and hollering. . . . still they made him ride that thing for the full time. When he was done, they found out what the problem was. The seat had fallen off his bicycle.

★   ★   ★   ★   ★

It took his mind off his heart problem.

Following is the same monologue as I would rewrite it for my own style of presentation:

I just got out of the hospital. I had everything I needed when I checked in— Money, my insurance forms, and the clean underwear that my mother always told me to wear in case I went to the hospital.

★   ★   ★   ★   ★

There were three things my mother always told me: Be a good boy, say my prayers each night, and always wear clean underwear in case I have to go to the hospital.

★   ★   ★   ★   ★

But you know something? I almost wish I hadn't. I'm dying to know what they do with people in the hospital who don't have clean underwear.

★   ★   ★   ★   ★

. . . this would have been my chance to find out.

★   ★   ★   ★   ★

. . . well, maybe next time.

★   ★   ★   ★   ★

I had heart surgery. In fact, the doctor who did my surgery is at this banquet tonight. I was pleased to see him until I glanced over at him during the meal and saw that his wife was cutting his meat for him.

★   ★   ★   ★   ★

But the surgery was the easy part—for me anyway, if not for my doctor.

★   ★   ★   ★   ★

After that they made me go to Cardiac Rehabilitation classes three times a week. That was tough. At this time in my life, it's difficult for me to do anything three times a week.

★   ★   ★   ★   ★

The people in that department are tough. I had this one nurse who was known as the "Mr. T of RNs."

★   ★   ★   ★   ★

★ ★ ★ ★ ★

Yeah, she has a black belt in nursing.

★ ★ ★ ★ ★

I'll tell you how tough they are: If I ever need a heart transplant, I'm going to get one from one of the people who work in Cardiac Rehab. I want to get one that hasn't been used yet.

★ ★ ★ ★ ★

We used to ride the stationary bike for a full half hour. This one guy was screaming and hollering. . . . still they made him ride. He screamed, he yelled. It didn't matter. They still made him ride that thing for the full time. When he was done, they found out what the problem was. The seat had fallen off his bicycle.

★ ★ ★ ★ ★

It took his mind off his heart problem, I'll tell you that.

A WORD BEFORE YOU START

You can see that I made some of these changes to improve the joke, and others simply to accommodate my speaking rhythm.

You will also learn that when you have questions about technique or style, you can always turn to those you admire. Listen to them and study what they do. It works for them; it can work for you.

Have fun with this research.

Chapter Eighteen

WORKING WITH TRANSITIONS

I had a teacher in high school who used to amaze all of us with his brilliance. Our curriculum included a leisurely walk after meals. A small group of students walked with a teacher and discussed topics of general interest. We were impressed by this particular teacher because no matter how remote the topic was, he always new the most minute details of it. We considered him a walking encyclopedia.

Later I learned that he used some mental "sleight of hand" on us. He had a trick. He would brush up on one particular subject and learn the most obscure trivia about it. During the walk he'd steer the conversation toward that topic. Though our talks seemed free-flowing, they were rigidly guided by this man.

He would cram for casual conversation.

That's the sort of control a monologist must wield over his audience. The person on stage must shepherd the thoughts of the listeners and guide them relentlessly in the direction he wants to go. Most importantly, though, the guidance must feel natural—unrehearsed.

That is the purpose of transitions in the monologue. They lead the audience effortlessly from one topic or subtopic to the next. They keep the monologue conversational.

If my teacher had tipped his hand that he had studied before our walk and was going to show off by leading us in the direction he wanted, we'd have labeled him a fraud instead of being awed by him. If comedians are too obvious in guiding the audience in a certain direction, their listeners become suspicious, too.

Even though we know that comics write and rehearse their material beforehand, we like to be deceived. We like to feel that their comments are "top-of-the-head" ad-libs. Smooth, relaxed transitions help the listeners believe that.

Transitions can take almost any form. Bob Hope sometimes announces a new topic simply by saying, "Hey, how about . . ." With that he's into it. We talked earlier about Henny Youngman's abrupt segues. They're so jarring that they've become a joke in themselves.

However, we're going to talk mostly about smooth transitions. We'll work on blends that you might find in normal conversation. We'll look for segues that are relaxed, almost invisible.

The best device for that type of blend is a joke, or at least a statement, that combines the elements of two topics—the one you're coming from and the one you're going to.

This creates almost an invisible seam in the comedy monologue. You're talking about your dog and how hungry he is. You mention that he bites the mailman, and suddenly you're into a discussion of how slow the mails are. It's painless, it's neat, and it helps your comedy feel effortless.

Just as we felt our teacher knew everything about everything, so the audience feels you can be funny about any topic that happens to pop up. And you can be—it's just that you, the comic, control what "happens to pop up."

Another consideration that helps transitions blend into the conversation is the routining of the monologue. By the routining, I mean the positions of the topics or the subtopics. They should be in logical order. If they're not, they're disturbing to the listeners. Often without even knowing why, the audience is distracted if the flow is illogical.

The logic can take many forms. It might be chronological. For instance, if you're talking about your new dog, you might start with spotting her in the pet shop window, making the purchase, bringing her home, recalling how she behaved that first night in new surroundings, and how she has misbehaved ever since.

Sometimes the logic is hierarchical. If you're doing a roast of a group of fellow workers, you might begin with the lowest in rank and work your way up to the highest.

Sometimes the order is determined by protocol. I once wrote a command performance show for a comic entertaining in a foreign country. I put the strongest material up front, but the comedian vetoed that order. Unfortunately, our funniest stuff was also our most incisive. The comedian correctly decided that we couldn't open with material that was the most critical of our host country. We could do that material only after we had first established a friendly sense of fun.

So routining is practically a seat-of-the-pants operation. You can use it in almost any order—provided it is logical.

I once watched a well-known comic do a nightclub act that was totally disjointed. He talked about his marriage, then about his travels to the west coast, then about his marriage, then about his medical problems, then about his marriage, then about his troubles with insurance companies, then about his marriage. It confused the audience, and it offended them. They felt that very little preparation had gone into his act. Jokes seemed to have been grabbed from a file drawer and thrown together. They were good jokes, but they weren't strung together in a believable flow.

Even the smoothest blends will be disruptive if they blend the wrong material. It's like weaving an invisible seam into carpeting only to discover that you've put different colors together. No seam will be invisible when you put a green rug next to a red one.

In Chapter Seventeen you got some practice in putting a monologue together. It should already be in logical order, but now you'll get some practice in blending topics and subtopics and making sure that the routine flows and feels relaxed.

= WORKOUT 18A =
"Column A—Column B"

A good transition joke takes ideas from two separate topics or subtopics. This workout is good practice for writing transition jokes because it gets you searching for similar and different characteristics in two separate ideas.

HERE'S WHAT YOU DO FOR THIS WORKOUT

1. Compile a list of 30 ordinary nouns. Arrange them into two columns of 15 nouns each.

2. Write at least five jokes that relate a characteristic from any noun in column A to a characteristic from any noun in column B.

HERE'S WHAT THIS WORKOUT WILL DO FOR YOU

This workout uses many of the skills necessary for good comedy writing. First you learn to search out characteristics and relationships between two words that seem to have no connection. Then you have to bond them together with your phrasing.

As your mind races through the lists of words, locating characteristics that unite them, you will be thinking funny—searching for the humor that unites them, as well.

HERE ARE SOME EXAMPLES

Here is an abbreviated list of six words and a couple of the jokes that I formed from them:

Food	Ring	Boat
Paint	Car	Floor

1. I put together "Food" and "Floor" for this gag:

   "I make biscuits that are so bad you can't eat them. But it's not a total waste. I did tile my bathroom floor with them."

★   ★   ★   ★   ★

2. I used "Ring" and "Boat" to write this joke:

   "My wife wanted a diamond ring for our 25th wedding anniversary and I wanted a boat. So we compromised. We bought the ring, but I get to scrape the barnacles off it whenever it needs it."

A WORD BEFORE YOU START

These examples show how you can find elements from practically any sector, analyze them for similarities and differences and then write a joke bringing these two facets together.

Have fun with this workout. It's especially practical.

WORKOUT 18B

"From Topic to Topic"

This exercise is even more practical than the last one. That was good practice in creating transition lines. It showed you how you could extract elements from two separate categories and write them into one joke, bringing the divergent elements together.

In this workout, you do the same thing with actual topics.

HERE'S WHAT YOU DO FOR THIS WORKOUT

1. Collect ten headlines from your daily newspaper. They can come from any part of the paper—the front page, the entertainment section, the sports pages, even the obituaries. They can be major headlines, but they don't have to be.

2. Arrange them in an order that you think will provide a logical, conversational flow.

3. Write transition lines that will take you smoothly through all ten of your topics. Assume that you have all the jokes you need on each topic, but you are now writing lines that will blend smoothly from one routine to the next.

HERE'S WHAT THIS WORKOUT WILL DO FOR YOU

This is excellent practice in routining a monologue. You have to arrange your topics in a logical progression—one that will feel natural to the listeners.

Of course, you may want to change the order as you write the transition lines. If you come up with a great line that combines elements three and five, you may find it expedient to relocate element four. That's fine—provided it doesn't disrupt the logic of the monologue.

HERE ARE SOME EXAMPLES

For these examples, let me manufacture five generic topics that might appear in any day's newspaper.

1) Our President has economic meetings with Japanese businessmen.

★   ★   ★   ★   ★

2) A young actor, call him Daryl Goodface, is arrested for fighting with a news photographer who harassed him outside a Hollywood restaurant.

★   ★   ★   ★   ★

3) A 7'2" college basketball player from State University signed a professional contract for several millions of dollars.

★   ★   ★   ★   ★

4) A Washington politician, Senator John Doe, is involved in an alleged scandal with a showgirl.

★   ★   ★   ★   ★

5) Scientists announce that fertilizer may be used eventually as a cure for male pattern baldness.

I've decided to arrange them in the following order:

1) The President and Japan first. Why? Because it's the biggest story of the bunch.

★   ★   ★   ★   ★

2) Next I'll go to Senator Doe's woes. It seems logical to keep the two political stories together.

★   ★   ★   ★   ★

3) Following that I'll put the routine about the actor, Daryl Goodface. That way we blend from scandal to scandal.

★   ★   ★   ★   ★

4) My fourth bit will be about the basketball player getting an exorbitant sum. No reason except that the next story is so whimsical compared to the others that it should be last.

★   ★   ★   ★   ★

5) The fertilizer being used for baldness. It seems separate from the other stories.

★   ★   ★   ★   ★

Here are the transition lines I might write for these five different elements:

(*Start with a few jokes about the President and the Japanese economy. Ending with . . .*)

". . . Having all that money is not always a blessing for a government. They have to figure out what to spend it on. Of course, we all know what Senator Doe would spend it on."

★   ★   ★   ★   ★

(*Then the few jokes on Senator John Doe and his problems, followed by . . .*)

"No matter how bad things may seem for Senator John Doe, they could be worse. He could have been taking a picture of Daryl Goodface at the time."

★   ★   ★   ★   ★

(*Then the jokes about Daryl the actor and his legal problems. That would end . . .*)

"Goodface can afford to pay the fine, though. Actors are the richest people in the world. I mean for people who aren't 7-foot-2 and graduates of State University."

★   ★   ★   ★   ★

(*Then we do the jokes about this topic, ending with . . .*)

"This kid's agent says he's worth twice as much, but we all know that what agents say is the world's latest cure for baldness."

★   ★   ★   ★   ★

(*We're into the final routine about fertilizer curing baldness.*)

A WORD BEFORE YOU START

The order of these gags was arbitrary, remember. It was at the discretion of the writer. The order must be logical, but there is more than one form of logic. For instance, we could have gone from the economic meeting with the Japanese to the basketball player signing. Both of them have to do with money. That's fine. However, the blend line would have to be changed. It might now read:

"It's hard to imagine how Japan could get so wealthy, especially since none of them can dunk a basketball."

These lines may not be the strongest in your monologue. They don't necessarily have to be. They are designed to keep the logic flowing.

Certainly, you should make them as powerful as possible, but the real strength of your monologue is in the comedy of your routines. These transitions jokes get you into your routines, and those routines should lead to the climactic jokes.

Have fun with this workout, and give it a lot of thought and effort. It can help your writing tremendously.

= WORKOUT 18C =
"From Subtopic to Subtopic"

This workout is practice in blending from subtopic to subtopic. These are more closely related than major topics are, but they're also a little more delicate. The blend has to be somewhat more subtle.

HERE'S WHAT YOU DO FOR THIS WORKOUT

1. Refer back to the list of subtopics you generated in Workout 9B. Select three of those five for further work.

2. Arrange those subtopics in a tentative logical order.

3. Write transition lines that move your monologue smoothly from subtopic to subtopic.

HERE'S WHAT THIS WORKOUT WILL DO FOR YOU

This is good practice in making those little blends within a monologue. The subtopics are already closely related, but subtle transitions keep the routine flowing in the direction you want it to go.

It is also a lesson in preparation. You created this list of subtopics, now you have to interrelate them. Eventually, you'll learn to think about this when you create the list to begin with. As we say when clients ask us for ideas for monologue topics and subtopics, "If you can't write the routine, don't submit the topic."

HERE ARE SOME EXAMPLES

Referring back to Workout 9B, my topic was "bringing home a new puppy," and I created this list of subtopics:

- a) how much it wets
- b) how much it eats
- c) how much it whined the first night
- d) how quickly you fall in love with it
- e) how quickly it gets its own way
- f) how it's more trouble than children

Now to refine it into a logical monologue, I'll rearrange the subtopics into this order:

- a) how quickly it gets its own way
- b) how it's more trouble than children
- c) how much it whined the first night
- d) how much it wets
- e) how much it eats
- f) how quickly you fall in love with it

With that order established, these are the transition lines that I wrote:

(*a to b*)

"That dog has me wrapped around its little finger. It can get anything out of me it wants. It's exactly the way children are for—oh, let's say, the first 30 to 35 years."

★　★　★　★　★

(*b to c*)

"You know, my children woke me up every couple of hours their first night at home, too. I didn't get mad at them, but I get mad at the dog. Of course, my children weren't chewing the couch apart at the time."

★　★　★　★　★

(*c to d*)

"All the thing did all night was whine and wet. I couldn't decide which end of it I hated more."

★　★　★　★　★

(*d to e*)

"I couldn't figure how so much liquid could come from such a little puppy. The next day she showed me. She ate $82 worth of dog food."

★　★　★　★　★

(*e to f*)

"She eats more than she's worth, she wets, she has accidents, but I love her. I think I love anything around the house that has more bad habits than me."

★　★　★　★　★

A WORD BEFORE YOU START

I think you can easily see how these transitions allow the comic to do four, five, or more lines about each subtopic and have the entire routine feel conversational. Each subtopic seems to flow out of the one that went before it.

Remember, too, that the order of the subtopics is arbitrary. If they are changed for whatever reason, the transition lines would have to change too.

That's the purpose of the transitions—to direct the flow of the conversation along whatever lines you decide.

Have fun with this workout.

= WORKOUT 18D =
"Smoothing Out the Monologue"

This workout will give you a practical, hands-on application of the transition. In this you will judge for yourself where a better transition is needed, what kind is required, and how to write one.

HERE'S WHAT YOU DO FOR THIS WORKOUT

1. Refer back to the monologue you composed in Workout 17C.

2. Reread it and analyze the transitions from subtopic to subtopic. The transitions were the only part of the rewriting and polishing process that we omitted in Chapter Seventeen.

3. Redo any transitions that seem abrupt or write transitions where you feel you need them.

HERE'S WHAT THIS WORKOUT WILL DO FOR YOU

This workout is good practice in finalizing a complete monologue. When you rewrote your monologue in the workouts in Chapter Seventeen, you may have intuitively inserted the blends that you felt were required. Fine. Then you'll have nothing to do here except approve the decisions you made then.

However, you may also see from this workout that even a completed, rewritten, polished monologue may have logic gaps, places where a less abrasive blend is required.

HERE ARE SOME EXAMPLES

I have no examples to offer here. This is your monologue and you'll spot the places where new lines are needed.

A WORD BEFORE YOU START

This workout is good training in spotting trouble spots and providing better lines.

Have fun with it. When you finish, you'll have a good, solid, beginning-to-end monologue to your credit.

Chapter Nineteen

WORKING WITH STORY PLOTTING

Most comedy writing in television today is in the form of situation comedies—"sitcoms" for short. Those are the shows that have a story line, as opposed to a variety format. *The Carol Burnett Show* was a variety show. There was no story, except for the brief ones within the sketches. *Cheers*, on the other hand, is a sitcom. Each episode tells a different story, but with the same central characters and usually the same setting.

A story written for a sitcom—or for a play, a dramatic film, a novel, or a short story, for that matter—must have a plot. A plot, very basically, is the sequence of happenings, the flow of events.

A monologue doesn't need this orderly sequence, but it can have it. For instance, Woody Allen used to do a monologue about taking a moose to a party. It progressed from one point to the next. In a sense, it was a short story. However, a monologist can also speak about current events and touch on them in almost random sequence.

As we saw in the previous chapter, a monologue should have a logical, conversational flow. A plot, though, must have a logical and *chronological* order, even though you don't have to tell it in that order.

A plot can jump forward in time or flash back, but it must tell a story logically. It can't be random. A plot must have a beginning, a middle, and an end.

A good plot is necessary for two reasons. First, it enables you to tell the story. And it helps the viewer to understand the story you're trying to tell. That's why it has to take on a logical sequence—not necessarily chronological, but logical.

Secondly, a good plot makes the story more interesting. In a book, it makes you want to turn the page, read the next chapter. That's why they say of a well written book that once you get into it, it's hard to put down. In a play, film, sitcom, or sketch, the plot makes you want to see how the story ends.

The first element of a good plot is the premise. It must be about something. Just as you can't write a joke until you decide what you're going to write about, you can't construct a plot until you know what your premise is. It will help your writing if your premise is well defined—to you, the writer.

It's a good idea to be able to express the basic premise of your story in one or two simple sentences. That will keep your mind focused on the story you're trying to tell, and that in turn will keep your story-telling focused, too.

Telling a story is different from living a story. In life, we can't escape the chronological ticking of the clock. We have to live day before night. Also, we can't escape 100 percent of the details. In telling a story we can and must eliminate non-essentials.

For instance, when you walk into a restaurant in real life, you see all the people who are in there. One person at table A may be wearing a brightly-colored plaid jacket, another at table B may be wearing a tuxedo, and so on. However, not all of these people are important to your story.

So when you tell about meeting someone at a restaurant, you wouldn't and shouldn't describe every person you pass while getting to your table. They're not essential. We do, however, want to know everything about the person you're meeting—or at least, everything about the person that's important to the story.

It's easier for you to know which elements of your story and its ambience are essential and which are not if you have a well-defined statement of your premise.

The second element of a good premise is interest. You are telling a story; therefore, you want people to listen. To be a good story-teller, you have to make the audience want to listen. You have to get them so involved in your story that they can't put the book down, leave the theatre, or turn off the TV until they find out how everything "turns out."

An intriguing plot accomplishes that.

One thing that makes a story interesting is unexpected complications. A good plot is a well-stated goal with obstacles to its attainment, and the solutions to those obstacles are found along the way. Hollywood supposedly likes happy endings, but you need plenty of frustration en route in order to have something to be really happy about at the end. It's those problems and the response to them that keeps the audience intrigued.

The third element is credibility. Your plot should be believable. That doesn't mean you can't write science fiction where the circumstances might be far from our present knowledge of reality. It doesn't mean you can't write comedies where the action is zany and silly. It doesn't mean you can't create dream sequences where time and space become confused and abstract. It simply means that each of the elements of your story must fit within a certain range of believability. Why? Because that supports your premise.

In *Back to the Future*, Michael J. Fox journeys back in time and influences the life of his own parents. I'm not sure I believe that would ever happen, but I did believe that it might happen, and it was told in such a way as to support that premise.

If however, parts of your story are totally unbelievable within their own context, you destroy the whole thing. It's like pulling one card out of a house of cards. The entire structure crumbles.

The film, *The Exorcist*, had several things in it that were unbelievable—the young girl's head spun around; she spoke in different languages and voices; she could change the temperature of the room at will. Nevertheless, these events were consistent with the story that was being told. It was about a phenomenon that stretched the imagination, therefore, the elements of the story could stretch the imagination.

On the other hand, if you're telling a normal, everyday story and you have two people get on a bus in New York and get off the bus two hours later in Madrid, you have a serious credibility gap.

You can only get away with it if it's consistent with your story and you "explain it logically"—even if the logic is only *your* logic.

I can recommend two worthwhile books that might help you with plotting:

How to Write Plots That Sell by F. A. Rockwell (Contemporary Books, 1975).

Screenplay: The Foundations of Screenwriting by Syd Field (Dell, 1984).

= WORKOUT 19A =
"Story in a Nutshell"

This workout gives you practice in defining a plot premise.

HERE'S WHAT YOU DO FOR THIS WORKOUT

1. Collect five stories that you've seen in movies, read in books, or seen on television.

2. Express the plot premises of each story in one or two simple sentences.

HERE'S WHAT THIS WORKOUT WILL DO FOR YOU

This workout teaches you to reduce a plot to its basic premise, which will help you keep your writing focused on the essentials that drive your story forward.

It's good training in seeing the underlying reason for the story and understanding why the author has included certain elements and omitted others.

HERE ARE SOME EXAMPLES

Rocky: An apparent nobody gets one shot at being somebody. Despite the odds against him, he gives all he has to the effort, if for no other reason than to prove to himself his real worth.

Bull Durham: A ball player who loves the majors, but doesn't have the skill to make it, trains and educates a young player with magnificent ability who doesn't appreciate how fortunate he is. Though the old pro dislikes the kid and is jealous of him, it's his contribution to "the game."

A WORD BEFORE YOU START

Once you write your brief synopsis, review the story line of the plot that you selected. See if each scene says something that is in keeping with the one or two sentences that you wrote.

It's a good way of seeing why a story is told a certain way. Have fun with it.

= WORKOUT 19B =
"Platonic Plagiarizing"

This workout is practice in "paralleling." That means to "copycat" a basic plot idea using a different setting.

Plots are used over and over again. For example, *West Side Story* was an updated musical version of Shakespeare's *Romeo and Juliet*. The classic film, *The Hustler*, was about a young up-and-coming pool player who wanted to challenge and dethrone the reigning champ, Minnesota Fats. Put guns in their hands instead of pool cues and you have the plot of countless westerns—the young gunslinger wanting to shoot it out with the legend. The same premise has been repeated with basketball players, track stars, poker players, almost every type of competitor.

I'm sure you can think of other examples, too. *Jaws* was similar to *Moby Dick*. Some even claim that *Gunga Din* and *Front Page* are twin stories.

HERE'S WHAT YOU DO FOR THIS WORKOUT

1. Research and outline a favorite book, film, play, or television show.
2. Find a situation that might parallel it.
3. Create a new premise, paralleling the original, and outline it using the new characters and situation that you just generated.

HERE'S WHAT THIS WORKOUT WILL DO FOR YOU

This is excellent practice in learning how to plot a story line. In copying the masters you're using ideas that have worked. You're following a blueprint that's been proven and are simply applying it to a new setting. The author of that original piece did something right; you are learning good habits in paralleling it.

Paralleling is not plagiarizing. Often the new story will hardly be recognized when compared to the original. New settings will dictate different plot points. For instance, a young pool player challenges a pro much differently than a gunslinger challenges his opponent. Therefore the story changes.

The only thing that remains is the plot skeleton. All of us humans are built on the same basic skeleton, too, Yet we're all individuals, separate and distinct. So are stories that are overlaid on basic plot outlines.

HERE ARE SOME EXAMPLES

Here's an outline of a *Dick Van Dyke Show* that I'll parallel for another sitcom:

MASTER PLOT OUTLINE

First scene: Rob is trying to fix a toaster with Laura looking on. Jerry, the next door neighbor, comes in to return a movie projector he borrowed. He tells Rob it's getting run down; Rob says he'll buy another one when he gets the money. He says, "You know, they cost $425." Laura asks Rob for $25 so she can do some shopping. They kid about her spending, but he gives her the money.

In searching for a handkerchief, Rob discovers a hidden checking account book in

Laura's name. It's for $378.16—a considerable amount. Jerry wants to know why it's in Laura's name only.

Next scene: At the office Rob tells Buddy and Sally about Laura's "secret." It bothers him that it is secret. They try to comfort him and explain it away, but only make matters worse.

However, through their talk they discover that tomorrow is Rob's birthday. That's it! She's been saving for a gift. He agrees. She must be going to buy him the projector that he wants. However, she's $47 dollars short.

Laura comes in. She's been shopping and decides to stop in just to say hello. Buddy and Sally leave them alone. Rob finds an excuse to give her $47 for her shopping. He even throws in an extra ten so she can buy the leather case, too.

Next scene: When Rob gets home from work that evening he's like a kid waiting for his new toy. He sneaks looks all over the house, trying to find the package. Laura tells him to relax; his birthday isn't until tomorrow. He continues to look anyway.

Finally, Laura says, "If you're going to be this childish, I'll give you your gift tonight." She goes to get it and Rob starts preparing to plug it in and try it out. He gets out an extension cord and plugs it in.

Jerry comes in to borrow the "old" projector. Rob gives it to him as a gift. Jerry leaves.

Laura comes in with her gift. It's a sports shirt.

Next scene: In the office the following day, Buddy and Sally surprise Rob with a birthday gift. It's a movie screen to go with his new projector. Rob tells them he got a sports shirt.

Rob can't work because he keeps worrying about what the "secret" bankbook is for. He determines to confront Laura that evening and get to the bottom of this deception.

Next scene: That night in the Petrie bedroom, Laura tries to go to sleep as Rob paces. Finally, he pulls out the hidden bankbook and asks Laura what it's all about.

She says she just wanted some money of her own. He wants to know why. She confesses that she was saving up to buy him a really nice present—years from now. She wants to buy him a sports car. Her mother saved and bought her Dad a fully furnished den on their 25th wedding anniversary. She wanted to do the same, but now Rob has ruined the surprise.

Rob is satisfied that she wasn't hiding anything from him and loves her all the more for thinking of him.

They hug and all ends well.

PARALLEL PLOT OUTLINE

Using that same premise of suspected deception and thinking that it was for oneself, I devised this parallel plot for the sitcom *Cheers:*

First scene: The gang is in the bar discussing Boston's city-wide "Ugliest Bartender Contest." It's a charity fund-raiser sponsored by a local television station. People donate money as their way of voting for their favorite bartender. It's called the "Ugliest Bartender Contest," but it's really a popularity event. The money goes to a good cause, and the winning bartender gets an all-expenses-paid trip to Bermuda—for two.

Sam, Cheers' entrant, has been running very close to first for the entire event. The folks are trying to guesstimate how much money is in the jar. Finally, they make a bet and count the cash. It comes to $186. They put the money back in the jar and settle their bet.

Rebecca comes out and takes the jar.

Later she comes into the bar, calls the headquarters of the contest, and tells them she will personally deliver today's tally that totalled $115. She leaves with the cash.

Next scene: The regular patrons are discussing what just happened. Carla thinks Rebecca's a thief. Others feel she just miscounted. Sam thinks she is jealous and doesn't want him to have the trip.

Finally, they devise a plan to see if this will happen again the next night. They determine that Carla will see how much money Rebecca has in her purse when she comes in. They will tally all the money put into the jar. Then they will see how much she leaves with at the end of the night and what she reports to headquarters.

Next scene: We see the cloak-and-dagger activity of the patrons trying to distract Rebecca so Carla can get to her purse. Eventually, they get their input and discover that again Rebecca is short.

When she's leaving Sam mentions that he's been falling behind. She says, "Well, it's not over till it's over."

At another bar meeting Sam is now sure he has the solution. She's not stealing; she's holding back. She's delaying the suspense. Tomorrow, the final night, Sam will be the glorious come-from-behind winner.

Next scene: At the bar, several deliveries are made to Rebecca. They are all boxes from expensive clothing stores. Now everyone is convinced she's a thief except Sam. He's still positive that he will be the last-minute victor.

They all watch the final announcement on TV and Sam finishes second, behind some bartender from a bar across town.

Next scene: In Rebecca's office, which is loaded down with empty boxes from expensive clothing stores, Sam confronts Rebecca. They know they made more than she was reporting.

She confesses. She took money from the Cheers' jar and put it into this other bar's earnings. It all went to the same charity, anyway, and she didn't keep a cent. Sam wants to know why. She confesses she did it for him. She knew that his ego, even for a publicity stunt, couldn't stand being the "Ugliest Bartender." She did it to keep him from being hurt.

He's genuinely touched. They might even hug.

Then there's someone calling for Rebecca. She grabs her luggage. She's going off to Bermuda with the winner of the contest.

★   ★   ★   ★   ★

Here are several other recognizable plots and how I might change them to generate new stories:

THE GUNFIGHTER PLOT

A youngster is trained by a legendary gunfighter. The kid practises until he feels he's the fastest gun in the west. The only way to prove that, though, is to challenge his mentor to a shoot-out. He uses every trick he can to outmaneuver his teacher. He makes sure the older gunfighter has had some drinks before issuing the challenge; he arranges the duel so that the sun is to his back and in the eyes of the legendary gunslinger.

★   ★   ★   ★   ★

One variation on this might be a young, comedy club comic who idolizes a legendary performer, such as Johnny Carson. The youngster copies the Johnny Carson style, perhaps even writes for Carson's TV show and then has some success on his own.

He can't rest until he knocks Carson off the air. He tries every sort of underhanded trick he can think of to discredit Carson, including character assassination, blackmail, whatever. Along the way, he loses the friendship of some of the people who helped make him an up-and-coming comedy star.

Does he knock his idol off the air? I don't know yet. That will come as the outline unfolds.

THE HIGH NOON PLOT

The gunfighter, a former killer, vowed to the woman he loved that he would never again carry a gun. Then he's challenged and he has to face his antagonist or be known as a coward.

He decides that he must face the challenge even if it means losing the woman he loves.

★   ★   ★   ★   ★

This might be updated to be the story of a kid who used to belong to gangs. He became a hoodlum and served time in prison, but abandoned that life and reformed when he fell in love.

Now the police come to him and ask him to go undercover—to become a hoodlum again. They convince him he has to do this to save other youngsters from a way of life that will destroy them.

It would only be a one-time operation, but it might cost him the woman he loves.

A WORD BEFORE YOU START

You can see that each basic plot could generate any number of parallel plots, and more important, that each story would take on a personality of its own.

The comedian challenging the talk-show champ would hardly be recognized as the offspring of a western shoot-out story.

Yet, if the structure is sound in the first plot, it should be sound in the second, provided all the elements remain believable.

So have fun with this one. You may just come up with an outline that's worth developing.

= WORKOUT 19C =
"What Would Happen Next?"

Many stories fall apart because the characters do things that no one would ever do. They become either totally unbelievable or completely ridiculous.

Within reason life has a certain predictability to it. There may be a range of reactions to certain stimuli, but one of those variations is usually present. For instance, if a person wins the Wimbledon championship, that player will jump for joy, throw the racket, fall to the ground in joy, jump the net, or show some other kind of pleasurable reaction. You don't know what the player will do, but you can expect some show of emotion.

If the player takes out a cigarette and lights up, that would be a shock. It would make the headlines of every sports page in the world, if not the front page.

If you were to write that into a screenplay *without a reason for it*, you'd have a major glitch in your writing.

This flaw is especially common in comedy writing because we try to set up our punchlines. We try to force jokes into the situation, and to get the jokes in we have to get joke setups in. Sometimes, though, the setups, although they blend beautifully into the comedy punch, don't coincide with the action. We force the action to take an unnatural turn to accommodate our comedy.

This workout will help get you thinking along logical believable lines.

HERE'S WHAT YOU DO FOR THIS WORKOUT

1. Select any two of the following situations:

   a) You're involved in a minor automobile accident.

   b) You find you have the wrong briefcase. You must have exchanged briefcases with someone during your bus ride to work.

   c) You're getting a physical and your doctor collapses suddenly.

   d) In a case of mistaken identity, police officers come into your place of business and arrest you.

   e) Two menacing people are in your seats at the ball game. Even though you hold the proper tickets, they refuse to move.

2. Write a brief outline that would carry the situations you selected to their natural conclusions. You may add funny twists if you choose, but you don't have to. In any case, whatever steps you add should be logical and believable.

HERE'S WHAT THIS WORKOUT WILL DO FOR YOU

This is training in writing plots that are believable. Any comedy that you add to your writing should fit the characters and the plot, not the other way around.

This is also good practice in eliminating another potential flaw from your writing. That is the "Why didn't they just do this?" error. That's the question the audience asks when writers complicate a plot with problems that don't really exist or are easily corrected.

Let's say someone is watching a scary television show. He begins crying and saying, "I'm frightened. I don't know what to do. This show could scar me for life." Well, that may be true, but all he has to do is turn the set off. That solves the problem.

Then there are stories that have plot points that are supposed to generate suspense and intrigue, while all they do is confuse the audience. The viewers say, "Why don't they just . . ."

HERE ARE SOME EXAMPLES

Let me take a minor catastrophe as my example. I'm at a hotel dressing for an important formal dinner date, and discover that I packed a shirt with french cuffs, but no cuff links. I have no other dress shirt and apparently no way of wearing this one. I have to be at the dinner in about 15 minutes.

Here's what I might do next.

1. I would call a bellhop and ask him to come to my room immediately. (You know how, when they carry your luggage to your room, they always say, "My name is so and so. If there's anything you need, call me." So I call.)

2. However, I can't be late, so I can't wait forever for him. I call the front desk to find out if there's a store in the hotel where I might buy some cuff links. There is, I'm told, but it's closed.

3. I explain my situation and ask if someone in the hotel might have access to that store. They tell me that it's privately owned and no one has keys to it.

4. The bellhop arrives and I ask if he might be able to get me a pair of cuff links. He can't think of any way to do it. All of their uniform shirts are button sleeves. He suggests safety pins and will search them down if I need them.

5. I tell him that I don't really want to wear safety pins with a dress suit, but he'd better find me some as a last resort. He leaves.

6. I call back to the front desk just on the chance that they might have an emergency stash of cuff links on hand for other forgetful guests like me. They don't.

7. I search through my toiletries kit and around the room for anything that might be used to keep my shirt looking semi-assembled.

8. The bellhop returns. I'll even take the safety pins now. He had a better idea and acted on it. There was a convention downstairs and all of the men were wearing lapel pins. He talked them out of several. He runs them through my cuffs, attaches them on the other side, and I have passable "cuff links." He has a nice tip.

A WORD BEFORE YOU START

This is admittedly a minor trauma, and you may have thought of other possible solutions. Nevertheless, the progression here is logical and believable.

It's more plausible than tearing the sheets off the bed and making a new shirt from them or some such silliness. It's more believable than putting a tie on without a shirt and hoping no one will notice.

I think you see the difference. When the plot sequence is believable, the humor flows naturally from it. When it's not, it destroys your credibility.

Understand, again, though, that craziness can be incorporated into a comedy script if it is plausible. You can write practically anything if you can explain it reasonably within your script.

What you need to avoid is the illogical action that you try to pass off to the viewers as logical. That can get your writing into trouble.

Have fun with this workout.

= WORKOUT 19D =
"What's the Worst Thing That Could Happen Next?"

Complications add interest to a plot. In the previous workout, you followed a logical sequence. Logic and consistency, though, are not enough to rivet a reader or a viewer. There must be some suspense. There has to be jeopardy.

In this workout you'll practise introducing that element into your story. I call it the "What's the Worst Thing that Could Happen Next?" workout.

HERE'S WHAT YOU DO FOR THIS WORKOUT

1. Select any two of the situations from the previous workout. You can pick the same two you selected before or different ones.

2. Now, still maintaining believability, create a problem out of each situation. Create the "worst" possible thing that could happen next.

HERE'S WHAT THIS WORKOUT WILL DO FOR YOU

This is good training in writing interesting, suspenseful plots. Jeopardy is an essential part of story-telling. Without it you're simply relating facts, not drama. *And drama is not the opposite of comedy; it is a part of it.*

In any situation comedy show there is always some jeopardy. It heightens the humor. So in any story you tell—even a funny story—you need to look for trouble. You look for the worst thing that can happen.

The "worst" is a relative term. It can be anything from real physical danger to just a comedic annoyance, like a pitcher of cold water spilled on your lap.

HERE ARE SOME EXAMPLES

I'll stick with my premise from the previous workout. I am dressing to go to an important formal dinner and discover that I forgot to pack cuff links. I can't wear my french cuff shirt. What's the worst thing that can happen next? Well, here are several possible ideas.

1) I notice in the hotel bathroom there is a tiny complimentary sewing kit. I decide to sew the cuffs of my shirt together. So I set the shirt on my lap, and hastily sew away. When I stand and pull the shirt up, we discover that I've inadvertently sewn the sleeve to my trousers and in lifting the shirt, I tear a large hole in my tuxedo trousers.

—OR—

2) I search frantically through my suitcase for an extra pair of cuff links, but find none. I'm so angry that I slam the suitcase shut, catching the tail of my shirt inside the case. When I go to open it, it won't open. It's either jammed or locked shut.

—OR—

3) I call downstairs and they have the solution. They will send someone up with an extra set of cuff links immediately. I'm roaming around the room in my underwear and just open the door when I hear the knock. The person they sent up is a female. She's embarrassed and just drops the cuff links on the bureau. I didn't look at her when I admitted her. Now I notice as she's going out the door that it's a woman and now I'm embarrassed. I chase after her to explain, but she's running down the hotel corridor. I turn to go back to my room and the door has swung shut, locking me in the hallway in only my skivvies.

A WORD BEFORE YOU START

You can see that now each of the problems I've created calls for some sort of solution before the plot can progress.

That ties in perfectly with the next workout. Have fun doing this one and then move on.

= WORKOUT 19E =
"Plus and Minus"

In this workout you'll get a chance to develop the plot further. In Workout 19D, you practised complicating the situation. Now you'll have to solve the complication and then complicate that solution; solve the next problem and create a frustration from that. In other words, your plot will continue to roller coaster. You'll go from a plus situation to a minus situation and continue on that way—positive, negative, positive, negative—until the final resolution of the plot.

Many comedy films are built solely on this structure. The National Lampoon *Vacation* films starring Chevy Chase were. You can probably think of many others.

Even a highly dramatic and suspenseful film like *Fatal Attraction* was constructed mostly on this basis.

This workout is good practice in learning to complicate and resolve each segment of your plot. Let's call it the (+) and (−) workout.

HERE'S WHAT YOU DO FOR THIS WORKOUT

1. Create a beginning premise. It can be a simple situation. Select one of those presented in Workout 19C, if you wish.

2. Now create a "What's the Worst Thing That Could Happen Next?" plot point. This will be your (−) plot point.

3. Resolve that (−) and turn it into a seeming positive (+).

4. Now complicate that solution again turning it into a (−).

5. Continue to alternate the (+) and (−) until you finally resolve the plot. Come up with at least three of each.

HERE'S WHAT THIS WORKOUT WILL DO FOR YOU

This is great practice in writing fiction of any kind. If you analyze any novel, screenplay, teleplay, or even sitcom, you'll see this method utilized.

HERE ARE SOME EXAMPLES

My example is from a recent episode of *Cheers*. In this story, Rebecca is frustrated because she feels her marketing talents are not appreciated by the corporation she works for. She teams up with Norm and promotes him as house painter. When her marketing campaign lands one job, she is ecstatic. That's where we'll pick up the (+) and (−) outline.

(+) Rebecca is so buoyed up by the success of landing Norm his first assignment, that she gathers the courage to go to corporate headquarters, tell off the CEO, and resign.

(−) Norm loses the job. He realizes he has to get to Rebecca before she destroys her career. She's already in the CEO's office, so Norm hijacks a window cleaning platform outside the building and signals Rebecca from outside the office.

(+) Rebecca learns about the job loss before she tells off the boss and forfeits her job.

(−) She now plays the weak-willed employee and sheepishly says to the boss all the sycophantic things that he would want said to him.

(+) She turns to leave, but then realizes that she has been lily-livered. She determines that she will not leave the office a coward. She will say what she came to say. She turns and tells the boss off.

(−) After her tirade we know that she will be fired.

(+) But no! The boss admires her for having the courage to stand up to him. He offers her the position of Vice-President in charge of all corporate marketing. She starts Monday. She's thrilled.

(−) The FBI come into the office and arrest the boss for insider stock trading. They handcuff him and lead him away before he can notify anyone that Rebecca has been promoted.

In the end, she neither loses her Cheers job, nor is she promoted. Like all sitcoms, it ends exactly as it started.

A WORD BEFORE YOU START

This was only one small episode from a half-hour situation comedy, yet you can see how quickly the plot kept changing. It would resolve, then complicate, then resolve, then change again. It continually switched from good to bad, from positive to negative.

That's what really interesting storytelling is all about.

Give this workout a lot of effort, and have fun in the process.

Chapter Twenty

WORKING WITH STORY STRUCTURE

Any story you write has two structures. It must follow two sets of guidelines. One is an artistic form; the other a pragmatic composition. Both are important. These separate, yet interdependent structures, are most evident in architecture. An architect has to design a building that will be attractive, appealing to the eye. At the same time the architect wants an edifice that will remain standing. Consequently, the rules of both art and engineering must be considered.

Your story, too, must be captivating. It has to interest an audience. It must also be able to survive in the marketplace. As a selling writer, you must create a product that is both beautiful and practical.

A student once asked architect Richard Fuller whether he considered aesthetic values when attacking an engineering problem. He answered, "No. When I'm working on a problem I never consider beauty. I think only of how to solve the problem. But when I have finished, if the solution is not beautiful, I know it is wrong."

We writers are the opposite. We consider ourselves artists first of all. We want to find the creative solution—the practical be damned. But we can't.

Let me give you a down-to-earth example of what I mean. Recently, I wrote a song parody for a variety show. We were to shoot it on location. The routine consisted of a verse of a popular song, followed by a brief visual joke. The visual would only last about 10 to 15 seconds on screen. The entire piece consisted of about four or five verses and visual jokes.

Regardless of the brilliance of the writing or the hilarity of the routine, it was impossible to do. Why? Because it would have taken about half a day to set up the cameras, lights, and other equipment for each visual joke. Five of those would have taken at least two days out of our shooting schedule, which was only three days total. It would have given us less than a minute of air time and probably would have cost more than the rest of the show. Comedically, it was fine; practically, it was unrealistic.

We had two options. We could drop the bit entirely, or we could change the structure of it to better accommodate our time and expense budgets.

Artistic guidelines are real, but they're not as rigid as the practical ones are. Nor are they always so apparent.

I was very excited about one of the sketches I handed in on the first television show I worked on. I thought it was ingenious, but the producer's expression was pained as he read it. "We can't use this," he said. The artist in me rebelled. "Why not?" I asked. Some irritation showed in my tone. The producer was very gentle with me, though. He handed me the manuscript and said, "Read Jim's line on page 3." Jim was the star of the show. I read the line. He said, "Now keep turning the pages until you come to Jim's next line." By the time I stopped flipping pages I was on page 11.

Sentencing the star to eight pages on stage doing nothing but "catching flies," might be a practical flaw. (It was.) But it's also an artistic error to leave any performer on stage with nothing to say or do. I, the writer, had violated that form.

Solutions were possible. I could give Jim stage business, or add dialogue, or devise a way to get him offstage until I needed him again eight pages later.

The artistic structure is not a list of regulations. You can't find an artistic code written down somewhere the way you might find a building code. It's more a "seat-of-the-pants" set of regulations that you learn by study, observation, and experience.

It exists in television, screenplays, stage plays, and novels. The rules are real, but they are flexible. You can experiment with them. Going back to architecture, for example, aesthetic tastes may change. Art deco may be in one year and old-fashioned the next. The engineering rules won't change that much, though. Gravity will always have the same pull on your structure regardless of what year you design it.

The practical structure is more rigid in writing, too. A sitcom begins on the hour and ends at the half-hour. You have to leave time for commercials whether the artist in you agrees or not.

On television, commercial spacing often determines the form of the show. Does that TV show have a short opening, a commercial, a long first and second act separated by commercials, and then a short closing segment? Does it have three acts of relatively equal length with commercials between? You can learn that by watching the show and observing.

A stage play is limited by the number of sets you can get in place on stage. A film can jump from location to location.

A television show may have limited sets because it's shot on tape before a live audience. Another show may be able to have chase scenes because it's done on film with no audience.

Even novels have practical limitations because paper costs money. A publishing company might not want a 480-page illustrated children's book. It might not want a novel that only has enough action to fill 82 pages.

No agent can sell your screenplay if it will only generate a film that runs 26 minutes.

You, as a writer, have to channel your talents to suit the arena you're writing for. You need to study novels, joke books, films, variety shows, sitcoms—whatever medium you want to write for. Each one of them has rules and guidelines. both artistic and practical.

The workouts in this chapter give you some guidelines for studying and analyzing many forms.

= WORKOUT 20A =
"Stop, Look, and Listen"

Each medium you want to write for has its own particular set of unwritten rules. You can absorb these by observation and experimentation. You watch and analyze, then you write. The more you write, the more you learn what works and what doesn't.

This workout will offer you a practical way to study certain writing arenas and learn from your studies.

HERE'S WHAT YOU DO FOR THIS WORKOUT

1. Watch two situation comedies currently on television. If possible, tape these shows for later review and to facilitate your note taking.

2. Do an outline of the stories, noting the approximate running time of each scene and where commercial breaks occur.

3. Watch an hour-long television show, preferably one with comedy overtones. Videotape this show for future study.

4. Do an outline of this show, noting the approximate running time of each scene and where the commercial breaks occur.

5. Watch a theatrical motion picture. Rent a video of it so that you can study it later and facilitate your note taking.

6. Do a scene-by-scene outline of the film, noting the approximate length of the scenes. (In television the length is important for practical reasons. In features, it may be important for artistic reasons.)

7. Read a well written stage play—a comedy—and, if possible, see a production of it.

8. From the script, make an act-by-act and scene-by-scene outline of the story. Running time is worth noting here again for both practical and artistic reasons. Read it aloud to get a feel for the running time.

9. Read a novel.

10. Do a chapter-by-chapter outline of the story.

HERE'S WHAT THIS WORKOUT WILL DO FOR YOU

In completing this workout, you'll be exposed to a lot of good writing, and you'll become more aware of the mechanics of it.

As you study and analyze each medium some of its unwritten rules of structure will come into focus.

Admittedly, many of these rules, because they are artistic, are nebulous. Nevertheless, as you concentrate on the structure of the pieces and study them, many of these principles will become more established in your mind.

A WORD BEFORE YOU START

There's plenty of work to do here, but it will be invaluable to your own writing. Give it your full attention, and have fun with it.

= WORKOUT 20B =
"Outline Your Story"

In the previous workout, you studied the creativity of other writers and the structure of forms in various writing arenas. In this workout, you'll get the chance to write a plot outline of your own.

HERE'S WHAT YOU DO FOR THIS WORKOUT

Select any one of the forms you've worked on —sitcom, hour-long television play, screenplay, stage play, or novel—and develop a plot outline based on one example in Workout 20A. Choose one that you can use later as your guide in writing a completed manuscript.

HERE'S WHAT THIS WORKOUT WILL DO FOR YOU

You'll develop many of your writing skills. By following the form you studied in the previous workout, you'll be writing to practical guidelines. In developing a story that you would like to write, you'll surely be exercising your creative and artistic talents.

HERE ARE SOME EXAMPLES

Your work will provide all the impetus you need. The shows you've watched and studied are the examples.

A WORD BEFORE YOU START

This is a heavy workout that demands dedication, but have fun with it. It's worth the effort.

Chapter Twenty-One

WORKING WITH PRODUCTIVITY

When I used to work on television variety shows, I met many of the top musicians. We had live orchestras then. Two things impressed me about these artists. First, they were ready to go at a moment's notice. They would come to the studio, read the music, and be able to play it almost instantaneously. That may not impress other musicians, but it did me.

Second, they could play all styles of music. That makes sense, doesn't it? You can't make a living doing variety shows without being able to play a variety of music. If a country-and-western singer was a guest, they'd play the accompaniment. If a classical musician was a guest, they'd play in that style. They were versatile. They had to be.

Comedy writers need these same abilities.

Deadlines are a part of writing. They usually require that you work a little faster than you'd like, and they mean that you don't have time to wait for inspiration to visit—you have to go and find inspiration. If necessary, you have to manufacture the inspiration.

The workouts in this chapter are practice in both getting the paper into the typewriter and getting it out of the typewriter and delivered to the client.

= WORKOUT 21A =
"Read and Write"

This workout is practice in using research to generate inspiration. The idea is that the more you know about a topic, the more chance you'll have of finding something interesting to write about.

HERE'S WHAT YOU DO FOR THIS WORKOUT

1. Select any five of the following places:

a) Paradise Island in the Bahamas
b) Philadelphia, Pennsylvania
c) The University of Michigan campus
d) Pensacola, Florida
e) Green Bay, Wisconsin
f) Waco, Texas
g) Stockholm, Sweden
h) Victoria, British Columbia
i) Halifax, Nova Scotia
j) Winnipeg, Canada
k) Elizabeth, New Jersey
l) Omaha, Nebraska
m) Hartford, Connecticut
n) Knoxville, Tennessee
o) Columbus, Ohio
p) Annapolis, Maryland
q) Santa Fe, New Mexico
r) Wilmington, North Carolina
s) Sydney, Australia
t) The Azores

2. Assume that you or a client of yours is going to speak at these places. You are to find as much as you can about each place you select, and then write three opening jokes that would be apropos for that place and the people who live there.

HERE'S WHAT THIS WORKOUT WILL DO FOR YOU

Earlier we said that you can't write about a topic until you have something to say about it. This workout is good practice in finding out enough about a topic—in this case a place—so that you have something to say about it.

You will also discover from this workout that when you learn about a topic, you'll *want* to say something about it. The knowledge generates the enthusiasm—the inspiration.

HERE ARE SOME EXAMPLES

In preparing material for comedians who travel all over the world, we often have to write about places we've never even heard of before. Here are a few tricks we use to do our research—research that eventually leads to gags.

Usually, we have a contact person—someone from that city who is arranging the details. We call and ask questions. We ask about places of interest, sports teams and well-known sports rivalries, well-known people in the area, and we ask what the headlines are in the papers.

A call to the local newspaper office is helpful. Librarians in the area are often generous with information, too.

The Chamber of Commerce is a possible source, but you have to be sure that the facts they supply are known by the general population. Sometimes their information can be too esoteric.

If there are colleges in the area, the sports information office is helpful, as are students who work on the school paper.

Also, check an atlas to find out exactly where the place is and what it's near; an almanac to find out some general information about it, and an encyclopedia for the same reason. The generalized information might prompt you to remember something about the area that you knew but had forgotten.

For instance, on a recent show that I wrote for, I read some background information on the locale and discovered that it had been a hiding place for pirates. That opened up a whole new area of joke writing for me. I had known it was a favorite port of pirates, but somehow just neglected to include that in my writing. This reading jogged my memory.

We also investigated personal friends. We'd find out if somebody had a friend who knew a friend who had a relative in the particular place. If they did, we'd call.

But you'll invent your own ways of gathering information and using that information to write sharp, incisive, funny material.

Have fun with this workout.

= WORKOUT 21B =
"Write and Write"

This workout will help you get to the keyboard when the writing muse is out to lunch. It can help to cure "writer's block."

HERE'S WHAT YOU DO FOR THIS WORKOUT

1. Insert a blank sheet of paper into the typewriter with no particular premise in mind for your writing.

2. Begin writing on any topic that comes to mind. Just write in a "stream of consciousness" style until you have filled about three quarters of the page with double-spaced typing.

3. Now stop and review what you have written. Use some part of your writing to generate a comedy idea—a premise for a monologue, a sketch, or a story.

You needn't complete the writing, but at least satisfy yourself that you have a workable idea that could be developed further.

4. Redo this workout three times.

HERE'S WHAT THIS WORKOUT WILL DO FOR YOU

This workout will prove to you that one cure for "writer's block" is writing—just getting something on paper.

A major reason for "writer's block" is fear. You fear you won't be able to complete the project, so you never start it. By writing something—anything—you distract your mind from this negative thinking. That allows your mind to do what it really wants to do—think about the premise.

HERE ARE SOME EXAMPLES

It's hard to illustrate this process; it's too individualized and personal.

This workout may seem awkward at first. Your first few sentences may be self-conscious; then you will find that you get into the flow of the writing. Your mind begins to hone in on one idea and you begin to expand on it.

If that happens, fine. If it doesn't happen, you will still be able to generate an idea when you reread your writing. The words on the page will force you to concentrate on what you've written and zero in with more focus on an idea.

Remember, you may not always get a finished product from this workout. You may get only the germ of an idea. You'll still have plenty of work to do to develop it into a workable premise. However, you will have started at least, instead of just staring at an idle keyboard.

Have fun with this one.

= WORKOUT 21C =
"Meet Your Quota"

This workout is practice in generating productive time. It's great preparation for meeting some of the "impossible" deadlines that all writers face sooner or later.

HERE'S WHAT YOU DO FOR THIS WORKOUT

1. Set an overall writing goal for one day. People write at different speeds, so you decide what your quota will be. Make it challenging but not overwhelming. If it's too easy, you won't reap any benefits; if its too difficult, you won't meet it and the workout will be discouraging rather than productive.

I would certainly not set a quota of less than five jokes per day.

2. Decide what your topic will be for the day—or for the week, if you want to tie each day's work together into a larger routine.

It might be a good idea to make this decision the day before you actually do the writing. There seems to be some magic in "sleeping on it." The body sleeps, but the mind seems to want to continue working through the night.

However, that's a personal choice. Just set aside a particular time to decide what you will work on for the upcoming day.

3. Schedule several times during the day when you will meet a quota of writing. This is apart from your normal writing agenda. This is the time you will "steal" from yourself. For example, you might set yourself a quota of one joke to be written while you're dressing in the morning. You might decide to write one joke before going down for breakfast. It might be appropriate to schedule two more lines at lunch. Perhaps a walk after dinner would be a fine time to think of a couple of lines.

Analyze your own day and set your own quotas. Again, they should be fairly leisurely—but not ridiculously so.

4. At the end of the day, assemble all these lines into some semblance of order. Continue this workout for five working days.

If you find it particularly useful, redo it several times.

HERE'S WHAT THIS WORKOUT WILL DO FOR YOU

This will prove to you that your mind can be working even while your body is doing other things. You may be able to write even while you're relaxing.

In any case, it will prove to you that you can find time to get some work done even when you're pressed. It may not seem like much, but it can add up and make the meeting of a difficult deadline just a little easier.

HERE ARE SOME EXAMPLES

No examples are needed here. It's important, though, to note that this is not necessarily a recommended writing practice. You may be cramming too much into an already crowded writing schedule. After all, there are times when relaxation—and getting away from creative thinking—is actually more productive than writing is.

Don't overwork yourself with this one, but push yourself a bit. Even though you are stretching your limits a little, have fun with it.

= WORKOUT 21D =
"Flying On Instruments"

As a professional writer, you'll often get writing assignments that aren't too thrilling. They may be things you either don't know anything about or don't care anything about—frequently, both. However, you have to finish the assignment. As one writer said about his assignments for a comedian client, "I can turn in great material or I can turn in terrible material. I can't turn in no material."

This workout is practice in researching and writing about topics that you probably know little about. They will be topics that come at you from the blind side. We've designed the workout so that you can't know in advance what you'll be writing about.

HERE'S WHAT YOU DO FOR THIS WORKOUT

1. Select any two numbers at random from one to eight.

2. The first number will represent the page number of the front section of your morning newspaper. Turn to that page.

The second number will represent the column on that page.

For example, 6–4 would mean that you will turn to page six of the front section of the paper, and select an item that is written in column four. That will be your topic for the writing you will do.

3. Read the complete article, making notes about interesting points, and write at least five jokes on the topic.

4. Redo this exercise at least five times—if not daily, perhaps every other day for a couple of weeks.

Note: You're not limited to just what is printed in column four. If the article begins on column one, or on another page, you can use all the information in the same article.

Most newspapers are designed so that there is more than one item in the selected column. We'll be nice and let you select any one of them.

HERE'S WHAT THIS WORKOUT WILL DO FOR YOU

This workout will be good practice in generating funny material on practically any subject. It's also good training for generating enthusiasm for any topic.

An added benefit, too, is that it may force you out of cliché topics. For a long time comics spoke mostly about their mothers-in-law, or their lazy brothers-in-law, or about fat people, or bald people. These topics became very "easy."

We have different subjects today, but many of them are becoming cliché, too. Young comics especially talk about drugs, dating, and sex. This workout will force you to look for and create humor in other areas. It's invaluable training.

HERE ARE SOME EXAMPLES

Examples would serve no purpose here. They would merely be a collection of jokes.

A WORD BEFORE YOU START

I would caution you not to surrender too soon on this workout. You may come up with some strange premises. Do them anyway. If you come up with advertisements, make that product or service your assignment. Every once in a while you might come up with a page and column that yields only difficult, almost impossible, premises. That's all right. Try them anyway. You may discover ways of bridging from an impossible topic to one that you can work on. You may need to force yourself to be a little deceptive, but it will still help you learn to be productive.

What I mean by bridging from one topic to another is sneaking a relationship into the premise that isn't there naturally (see the section on transitions, pages 151–159). For example, suppose the topic you wind up with is neutralization of negative particles by the ionization of atmospheric magnetic interwaves. Okay? How do you do a joke on that subject? Well, you could say:

> "The only way I know to neutralize negative particles is to get Dean Martin to breath on them for me."

★   ★   ★   ★   ★

> "Dean can neutralize anything. His burp can stop a mad rhino in mid-attack."

You see, you've taken some obscure subject and related it to something you know. Tricky, but sometimes necessary. Even that, though, is good comedy writing practice.

Have fun with it.

Chapter Twenty-Two

WORKING WITH CREATIVITY

Laugh-In was a bright, innovative, entertaining show when it debuted in 1968. I worked on the show during the 1971–72 season, one year before it went off the air. Each week, my family would watch the telecast, and my youngsters would be able to predict the punchline of almost every sight gag.

When *Laugh-In* was fresh and different it was funny. Eventually, though, the format became predictable. When it was predictable, there was no surprise, consequently no humor.

Humor has to change. It has to keep flowing or it stagnates. As a comedy writer, you have to devote time and practice not only to being funny, but also to being creative, innovative. You not only have to invent new jokes, but new forms. You have to find new ways of being funny.

What new ways are there of being funny? That's difficult to say. It's like predicting the future. We know there will probably be different modes of transportation in the year 2089, but we don't know what they will be. Someone will probably discover or invent something that solves the problems of the gas engine automobile.

Comedy changes, too. In the early days of television there were true variety shows—burlesque or vaudeville—shown on the home screen. Ernie Kovacs began to use the electronics of the new media as a punchline. Many of his jokes could only be done on television. *Laugh-In* was an updated version of Kovacs's genius. Then variety shows practically disappeared; talk show formats replaced them. Who knows what will come next?

Monologues are different today than they were in vaudeville. The young comics work differently from the older ones. They add, they subtract, they change, and generate a whole new style. That will change, too.

A good humorist has to keep up with the times and get a step ahead of them. It's the creative innovators who reap the biggest rewards.

The workouts in this chapter will give you a little practice in being daring with your comedy. They'll goad you into trying something different—something that hasn't been done before—maybe even something that can't be done.

Nevertheless, there are benefits in trying. Creativity is a gift; but it's a gift that can be developed with practice.

So, these workouts may challenge you. Some of them may overwhelm you. That's all right. Just when you feel the most frustrated, you might find the solution. That's the way careers in comedy go, too. That brilliant idea may hit you just when you think it's never coming.

Have fun with these.

= WORKOUT 22A =
"Desk Spot"

Johnny Carson introduces some new forms of comedy on his show. The humor in his monologues is sharp and entertaining, but the form is traditional. There's nothing wrong with that. He does try different things in his "desk spots," though. The desk spot is the routine he does from his desk after the monologue. It might be captioning photographs, or "The Great Carnac," or coming up with new titles for old books. It might be anything, in fact. Sometimes these pieces work and sometimes they don't. That's the risk of innovation.

In this workout, we're going to ease into a creative form by asking you to design one for a traditional piece.

HERE'S WHAT YOU DO FOR THIS WORKOUT

1. Come up with a clever premise that might be used as a Johnny Carson "desk spot."

2. Once you formulate the premise, write at least five jokes as examples.

HERE'S WHAT THIS WORKOUT WILL DO FOR YOU

You're developing a new form of comedy—not simply writing jokes or situation comedy premises. You're actually inventing a new idea.

Since that is the premise of this workout, it would be bending the rules to simply rewrite a "desk spot" that Johnny Carson has already presented. For instance, it would be wrong for the purposes of this workout to just write new jokes for the "Great Carnac" routine.

HERE ARE SOME EXAMPLES

One idea that I might invent would be to take some black and white photographs or drawings and do some doctoring of them with a red ink pen. For example:

I can see a picture of some swashbucklers. One of them has the red ink running down his leg. The caption might read:

"Excuse me, Captain, but I think you should be more careful when you're putting your sword into your scabbard."

★ ★ ★ ★ ★

Another might be a picture of a gentleman whose eyes are colored bright red. The captain could say:

"I take it sir that's the first Bo Derek movie you've ever seen?"

You get the idea.

Another idea would be to doctor some classical pictures, inserting celebrities into the scene. For example:

The classic painting "American Gothic" (That's the one with the grim-looking couple standing side by side in front of their farmhouse. The husband holds a pitchfork.) with Tammy Bakker looking over the wife's shoulder saying:

"Can I borrow that pitchfork? I have to adjust my eyelashes."

★   ★   ★   ★   ★

Or "Washington Crossing the Delaware" with Don Rickles in the boat, saying:

"Sit down, George. You're not the President yet."

I recently saw another good example of innovative comedy that is selling well. It's a book called *The 72 Toughest Holes in Golf*. It is a collection of photos of various places, that have been altered to become golf holes. For example, the authors doctored a Mt. Rushmore photograph to show the tees on top of George Washington's head and the green atop Teddy Roosevelt. They provided appropriate copy, also, giving a little background about this particular golf hole.

The book is funny, clever, and inventive.

A WORD BEFORE YOU START

The purpose here is to be creative, to be different. Once you create the form, the jokes will come. Concentrate on trying to come up with a totally original concept, not a rehash of something you've seen before or a variation on it.

It may not be easy, but it's good practice. Have fun with it.

= WORKOUT 22B =
"Comedy Parlor Game"

In this workout you'll try to have some fun having some fun.

HERE'S WHAT YOU DO FOR THIS WORKOUT

Create a new parlor game that uses some form of comedy creativeness as a basis.

HERE'S WHAT THIS WORKOUT WILL DO FOR YOU

This is a good exercise in creativity, and if you come up with a fun, workable game, it can be practice for your comedy writing, too.

HERE ARE SOME EXAMPLES

Here are some that might help you get started:

THE ANSWER GAME

This is a game I used to play at work long before Johnny Carson began doing the "Great Carnac." Several of us would submit cliché sayings and pass them around. Then about a week later we would all submit questions that would produce the clichés as answers.

For instance, one cliché was "A Hole in One." The question that someone submitted to win that one was, "When Frank Ford met the James brothers, what did he leave?"

★　★　★　★　★

TRIVIAL COMEDY

This is a variation on the popular board game, "Trivial Pursuit." We would play it with the same cards and questions except that whoever had the funniest answer would win the round. The other players would vote on the best comic reply. It's challenging and it's fun.

★　★　★　★　★

THE COMEDY WORD GAME

Here we would either hand out cards with words printed on them, or go to page numbers in the dictionary and select words. Players would then submit jokes made from as many of the words as they could. If the group accepted the joke, the player would hand in those cards. If not, the player would have to select more words. The object of the game would be to get rid of all the cards. No, I should change that. The object was to have fun and to write a few crazy one-liners in the process.

A WORD BEFORE YOU START

Again, the object here is to be creative. If the game is a winner and fun to play, that's a bonus.

= WORKOUT 22C =
"Do It Yourself"

This is the ultimate challenge to creativity. And a fitting last workout for this book.

HERE'S WHAT YOU DO FOR THIS WORKOUT

1. Create five new workouts to supplement this book and to help you improve your own writing.

2. Once you create the workouts, spend some time doing them.

HERE'S WHAT THIS WORKOUT WILL DO FOR YOU

The benefits here are whatever you want them to be —whatever you need most for your comedy writing.

HERE ARE SOME EXAMPLES

The workouts in this book are the examples.

Learning and writing seems easier when you're having fun. That's why I've ended almost every workout with that advice. Have fun.

PARTING WORDS

Someone once said there were only three ways to learn to write. They were to write, to write, and to write. If you've gotten to this point in the book and faithfully done all or most of the workouts, you've written, written, written. Like it or not, you're a better writer than when you started.

However, you're not done with this book. The workouts here will be valuable to you for as long as you want to be an excellent writer.

From time to time, some of your skills will require touch-up work, fine tuning. Go back and redo those workouts that will help. If the workouts are organized in a way so that the examples are exhausted the first time you do them, create or research new examples. That's an exercise not only in writing, but in creativity.

These workouts are the product of one author's imagination. Devise some of your own to improve different facets to your writing skills.

To learn to write you have to write, write, write; to be a good writer, you have to keep writing, keep writing, keep writing. Henry David Thoreau said, "I put a piece of paper under my pillow, and when I could not sleep I wrote in the dark."

ABOUT THE AUTHOR

Gene Perret is a self-taught comedy writer. He learned his technique by listening to Bob Hope monologues, typing them out, and trying to duplicate the style with different topics.

Gene's writing career actually began as an after-dinner speaker. He would write and perform his own material, and gained such a reputation that other performers began to buy the material that he presented.

Perret has written material for Phyllis Diller, and has been a staff-writer with Bob Hope since 1970. Today he is Hope's head-writer for the comedian's television specials and many personal appearances.

Perret has written in TV for such shows at *The Jim Nabors Hour*, *Laugh-In*, *The Bill Cosby Show*, *The Carol Burnett Show*, and others.

He produced and wrote *Welcome Back, Kotter*, *Three's Company*, and *The Tim Conway Show*.

Perret has earned three Emmy awards for his writing and one Writer's Guild Award.

He also publishes a newsletter about the comedy business for aspiring writers and performers called "Round Table."

INDEX